i

DEDICATION

I humbly dedicate this work to the supreme spiritual being.

TABLE OF CONTENTS

FOREWORD

Artificial intelligence is not merely a technological evolution. It is a fundamental shift in the way intelligence manifests itself in the digital age. The development of AI agents represents a critical juncture in human history, one that challenges long-held assumptions about cognition, autonomy, and decision-making. This book is not just a guide to understanding AI agents—it is a blueprint for those who seek to master the art and science of AI-driven intelligence.

As an industry leader in artificial intelligence, I have witnessed firsthand the staggering pace of innovation in this field. I have seen neural networks evolve from fragile, narrowly focused models into robust, adaptable architectures capable of performing tasks that once required human intuition. I have seen AI agents transition from simple rule-based systems to sophisticated autonomous entities capable of reasoning, learning, and even predicting human behavior. With each advancement, one question becomes increasingly urgent: What is the true potential of artificial intelligence, and how can we harness it responsibly?

The Dawn of Intelligent Agents

To understand the significance of AI agents, we must first revisit a pivotal moment in history. In 1950, Alan Turing posed a revolutionary question: *Can machines think?* This inquiry laid the foundation for artificial intelligence as a discipline. In the decades that followed, researchers such as John McCarthy, Marvin Minsky, and Herbert Simon developed symbolic AI, a framework in which intelligence was encoded as explicit rules and logical operations. This approach, known as Good Old-Fashioned AI (GOFAI), dominated early AI research, shaping expert systems and rule-based decision-making frameworks.

However, intelligence is not merely a set of predefined rules. The limitations of GOFAI became evident as researchers confronted the challenge of scaling rule-based systems to complex, unpredictable environments. The emergence of connectionist models, particularly artificial neural networks, provided a new paradigm. Inspired by the structure of the human brain, these models enabled machines to learn from data, uncover patterns, and generalize knowledge beyond their initial programming.

The evolution of AI agents has followed a similar trajectory. Early AI agents were deterministic, programmed with rigid rules governing their behavior. Today, agents leverage deep reinforcement learning, probabilistic reasoning, and multi-agent collaboration to navigate complex decision spaces. The shift from centralized control to decentralized, emergent intelligence represents one of the most profound transformations in AI research.

The Cognitive Architecture of AI Agents

At their core, AI agents are defined by three fundamental capabilities: perception, reasoning, and action. These capabilities mirror the cognitive functions of human intelligence, raising profound questions about the nature of artificial cognition.

1. **Perception** – AI agents must interpret raw data from the world. This includes computer vision for image recognition, natural language processing for textual comprehension, and sensor fusion for real-time environmental awareness. Advances in transformer architectures, such as OpenAI's GPT and Google's Gemini, have redefined how AI systems process information, enabling nuanced, context-aware understanding.

2. **Reasoning** – An AI agent must evaluate its environment, model uncertainty, and make informed deci-

sions. The integration of Bayesian inference, probabilistic graphical models, and deep reinforcement learning allows AI agents to navigate uncertainty with increasing sophistication. Judea Pearl's work on causal reasoning has provided critical insights into how machines can go beyond correlation to understand cause-and-effect relationships.

3. **Action** – The ultimate purpose of an AI agent is to act upon its environment, whether executing trades in financial markets, diagnosing diseases in medical applications, or optimizing supply chains in logistics. The implementation of autonomous decision-making frameworks enables AI agents to adapt dynamically to real-world challenges.

Beyond Supervised Learning: The Future of Autonomous Intelligence

A defining moment in AI history occurred in 2016 when AlphaGo, a reinforcement learning agent developed by DeepMind, defeated the world champion Go player Lee Sedol. This milestone was not just about a machine winning a game; it was about the emergence of agents that could develop novel strategies beyond human comprehension. Unlike traditional AI models that rely on labeled datasets, AlphaGo learned through self-play, refining its decision-making through millions of simulated interactions.

This shift toward self-supervised learning and autonomous adaptation represents the next frontier of AI agent development. Research in emergent intelligence suggests that AI agents, when placed in sufficiently complex environments, begin to exhibit behaviors that were not explicitly programmed. OpenAI's investigations into multi-agent reinforcement learning have demonstrated how AI agents develop negotiation skills, deception tactics, and cooperative strategies, mirroring behaviors found in biological ecosystems.

However, with great power comes great responsibility. As AI agents become increasingly autonomous, ethical considerations must remain at the forefront of their development. The risks of AI bias, adversarial manipulation, and unintended consequences must be addressed with rigorous safeguards. The alignment problem, as highlighted by Stuart Russell, underscores the need for AI systems to be designed with human values in mind.

Why This Book Matters

Mastering AI agents is no longer optional—it is imperative for anyone seeking to remain at the cutting edge of technology. Whether you are an engineer, researcher, entrepreneur, or strategist, the ability to understand, build, and deploy AI agents will define your competitive advantage in the coming decade.

This book provides more than just technical knowledge. It offers a deep, structured, and transformative learning experience that integrates:

- **Historical insights and foundational theories** to provide intellectual grounding.

- **Hands-on implementation guides** to bridge the gap between theory and practice.

- **Real-world case studies** demonstrating how AI agents are reshaping industries.

- **Cognitive and psychological frameworks** to enhance AI decision-making.

Each chapter will progressively build upon the last, ensuring a seamless learning journey from fundamental AI principles to advanced agent-based models. By the end of this book, you will not only understand AI agents—you will be equipped to create them, optimize them, and push the boundaries of their capabilities.

Artificial intelligence is not simply a tool. It is a force that will redefine industries, economies, and societies. The AI agents we build today will shape the digital ecosystems of tomorrow. Those who master AI agent development will not only navigate the future—they will define it.

The journey ahead will be challenging, but for those who dare to venture into the world of intelligent machines, the rewards will be extraordinary. Let us begin.

ACKNOWLEDGMENTS

The field of artificial intelligence stands as a testament to human ingenuity, perseverance, and the relentless pursuit of knowledge. This book would not have been possible without the intellectual foundation laid by the pioneers of AI, the researchers pushing the boundaries of computational intelligence, and the interdisciplinary minds integrating cognitive science, neuroscience, and mathematical rigor into machine learning.

First and foremost, I extend my deepest gratitude to the giants on whose shoulders modern AI stands. Alan Turing's seminal work, *Computing Machinery and Intelligence*, introduced the question that continues to shape AI research: *Can machines think?* His Turing Test remains a fundamental measure of artificial intelligence, challenging the field to develop machines capable of human-like conversation and reasoning.

Marvin Minsky and John McCarthy, the architects of Good Old-Fashioned AI (GOFAI), laid the groundwork for symbolic reasoning, knowledge representation, and heuristic search. Their efforts provided a structured framework for early AI, influencing expert systems and early problem-solving architectures.

Geoffrey Hinton, Yann LeCun, and Yoshua Bengio revolutionized AI through their contributions to deep learning. Their breakthroughs in backpropagation, convolutional neural networks (CNNs), and unsupervised learning have driven the shift from rule-based AI to data-driven intelligence. Without their work, AI agents would lack the adaptability and pattern-recognition capabilities that define modern machine learning models.

I am equally indebted to Judea Pearl, whose work on probabilistic reasoning and causal inference has reshaped how AI systems interpret uncertainty and causation. His research in Bayesian networks provided a bridge between statistical learning and reasoning, allowing AI agents to operate in ambiguous and complex environments.

This book also draws heavily from the advancements of Stuart Russell and Peter Norvig, whose seminal work, *Artificial Intelligence: A Modern Approach*, remains the definitive text on AI theory and application. Their contributions to agent-based models, reinforcement learning, and ethical AI development have guided much of the discussion within these pages.

Beyond the pioneers of AI, this book has been shaped by countless researchers, engineers, and visionaries at the forefront of AI innovation. The teams at OpenAI, DeepMind, Google Brain, Meta AI, IBM Research, and Microsoft AI have continued to redefine the limits of artificial intelligence through advances in self-supervised learning, adversarial networks, and reinforcement learning. Their whitepapers, research findings, and open-source contributions have provided invaluable insights into the evolution of AI agents.

The integration of cognitive psychology into artificial intelligence has been a critical aspect of this work. The insights of Daniel Kahneman, whose research on cognitive biases and decision-making informs AI-driven reasoning, have proven indispensable. Likewise, the work of David Marr in computational neuroscience has influenced AI perception models, offering a framework for understanding how machines process sensory information.

The philosophical dimensions of AI are equally essential. The works of Nick Bostrom on superintelligence, John Searle on the Chinese Room argument, and Ray Kurzweil's predictions on the singularity have provided critical perspectives on the trajectory of AI development. Their insights have helped shape discussions on the ethical, cognitive, and existential implications of artificial intelligence.

I also extend my appreciation to the broader research community contributing to AI safety, fairness, and interpretability. Organizations such as the AI Alignment Research Center, the Future of Humanity Institute, and the Partnership on AI continue to address the challenges of bias, robustness, and the long-term impact of AI on society.

This book is not solely the product of theoretical knowledge. It has been informed by real-world applications and case studies provided by industry leaders in finance, healthcare, cybersecurity, robotics, and autonomous systems. The contributions of professionals working in these fields have enriched the discussion, ensuring that AI agents are understood not just as theoretical constructs but as practical tools reshaping industries.

To the engineers and developers who have tested, refined, and deployed AI models in production environments, your work has been instrumental in shaping the methodologies presented in this book. The lessons learned from real-world implementation, from adversarial robustness to ethical AI considerations, have been integrated into every chapter.

Finally, I extend my gratitude to the readers. Your curiosity, ambition, and willingness to engage with AI at its deepest level are what drive the continued evolution of this field. The knowledge within these pages is meant to be a foundation— a stepping stone for your own research, experimentation, and contributions to artificial intelligence.

May this book serve as both a guide and an inspiration as you navigate the ever-expanding world of AI agent development.

INTRODUCTION

Artificial intelligence has reached an inflection point. What began as an abstract theoretical pursuit has evolved into the most transformative technological force of the modern era. From its earliest conceptualization by Alan Turing in *Computing Machinery and Intelligence* (1950) to the neural network renaissance led by Geoffrey Hinton, Yann LeCun, and Yoshua Bengio, AI has reshaped industries, economies, and the very fabric of human cognition.

Unlike previous technological revolutions that altered the way humans interact with the world, AI challenges something more profound—it redefines intelligence itself. The shift from symbolic reasoning (Good Old-Fashioned AI) to connectionist models (deep learning) has enabled machines to process language, recognize patterns, and even generate creative works. These advancements have moved AI from mere automation to autonomous decision-making, with systems such as DeepMind's AlphaFold solving decades-old biological puzzles and OpenAI's GPT-4 generating human-like text indistinguishable from expert writing.

The paradigm shift is not just about machines becoming smarter. It is about the augmentation of human intelligence. AI is no longer a tool used to optimize processes—it is a force that alters the way humans think, work, and solve problems. To thrive in this era, one must understand AI not just as a technological phenomenon but as a cognitive revolution.

You vs. AI: Why Understanding AI Agents is Your Competitive Edge

A fundamental misconception about artificial intelligence is that it exists merely to replace human effort. In reality, AI functions as an intelligence amplifier, extending human capabilities beyond conventional cognitive limits. Those who understand how AI operates—its strengths, weaknesses, and hidden biases—gain an unprecedented competitive advantage in every domain.

Consider financial markets. Algorithmic trading systems driven by reinforcement learning and adversarial networks now execute trades at speeds impossible for human traders. These systems do not operate in isolation. They interact within multi-agent ecosystems, competing and adapting in real time. Traders who understand the dynamics of AI-driven markets can anticipate shifts before they occur, leveraging machine intelligence as an extension of their strategic acumen.

In healthcare, AI-powered diagnostics, such as Google's DeepMind Health and IBM Watson, outperform human radiologists in detecting diseases like cancer. However, these systems remain fundamentally statistical in nature—prone to adversarial attacks and distributional shifts. Medical professionals who grasp the underlying mechanics of AI will not be replaced. They will be empowered, wielding AI as a diagnostic co-pilot that enhances clinical precision.

Cybersecurity presents another battleground. Autonomous threat detection systems, utilizing self-supervised learning, adapt to novel cyber threats faster than traditional security measures. However, adversarial machine learning exposes vulnerabilities in AI defenses, making knowledge of AI security indispensable for professionals in the field.

The ability to think alongside AI will be the defining skill of the next century. Those who fail to adapt will become obsolete, while those who master AI will shape the future.

How This Book Will Transform You: The Hidden Path to Mastery

This book is not just about artificial intelligence. It is about understanding intelligence itself—how machines think, how they learn, and how their evolution mirrors fundamental principles of human cognition. It will take you from foundational AI concepts to advanced agent-based architectures, providing both theoretical depth and practical application.

You will uncover the historical evolution of AI, from symbolic logic to deep neural networks, and explore the philosophical questions that continue to shape its development. More importantly, you will gain hands-on knowledge of AI agent design, reinforcement learning strategies, and real-world implementation techniques. Each chapter will immerse you in multi-sensory, intellectually stimulating narratives, reinforcing complex ideas through thought experiments, industry case studies, and practical frameworks.

This is not a passive reading experience. Every concept will be accompanied by real-world applications, enabling you to transition from theoretical knowledge to actionable intelligence. By the time you finish, you will not only comprehend AI—you will be able to wield it with precision, strategy, and foresight.

Your Journey from Beginner to Expert: A Psychological Blueprint for Success

Mastering AI is not merely an intellectual pursuit. It is a cognitive transformation that requires reshaping how you process information, solve problems, and interact with intelligence itself. The journey from beginner to expert follows a structured progression, deeply rooted in cognitive psychology and skill acquisition theory.

Stage 1: Unconscious Incompetence (The Illusion of Understanding)

At this stage, you may believe you understand AI because you have read news articles, experimented with ChatGPT, or seen deepfakes online. However, real AI expertise requires deeper immersion. You must recognize the gap between surface-level familiarity and true comprehension.

Stage 2: Conscious Incompetence (The Struggle of Learning)

As you dive into AI concepts—gradient descent, reinforcement learning, self-supervised models—you will encounter cognitive dissonance. The complexity may seem overwhelming. This is where most people abandon the pursuit, mistaking difficulty for impossibility. However, this struggle is essential for genuine mastery.

Stage 3: Conscious Competence (Structured Learning & Application)

At this stage, the principles of AI become clearer. You will understand the distinctions between GOFAI and connectionism, symbolic vs. subsymbolic reasoning, and centralized vs. distributed agents. You will begin applying these concepts in real-world contexts—training models, analyzing AI decision-making, and integrating machine learning into your workflow.

Stage 4: Unconscious Competence (AI as Second Nature)

At the final stage, AI knowledge becomes intuitive. You will no longer need to consciously think about the mechanics of backpropagation or attention mechanisms—they will be second nature. You will anticipate AI behaviors, predict its limitations, and innovate beyond existing frameworks.

This book is structured to guide you through this transformation. Each chapter builds upon the previous one, reinforcing layered learning methodologies to ensure long-term retention and deep comprehension.

You are entering one of the most intellectually demanding yet profoundly rewarding fields in human history. AI is not merely a tool—it is an extension of intelligence itself. The next pages will take you deeper into the principles of AI agents, exploring their cognitive architectures, decision-making frameworks, and real-world applications across industries.

Prepare to challenge assumptions, dismantle misconceptions, and think at the frontier of artificial intelligence. The journey ahead will not only redefine your understanding of AI but also transform the way you engage with intelligence itself—both artificial and human.

CHAPTER 1
Understanding AI and Intelligent Agents

Artificial Intelligence (AI) is no longer a concept confined to science fiction. It is an evolving field of study and engineering that has permeated nearly every aspect of modern life. AI refers to the simulation of human intelligence in machines that are capable of reasoning, learning, problem-solving, perception, and natural language understanding. At its core, AI seeks to create systems that can process information, recognize patterns, and make decisions—often at speeds and accuracies far beyond human capabilities.

The field of AI can be traced back to the pioneering work of Alan Turing, who proposed the Turing Test as a means to determine whether a machine could exhibit intelligent behavior indistinguishable from that of a human. His seminal work, *Computing Machinery and Intelligence* (1950), laid the groundwork for AI research. Following Turing, the advent of symbolic AI in the 1950s and 1960s, championed by researchers such as John McCarthy and Marvin Minsky, introduced rule-based systems that mimicked human logic through formal reasoning structures.

Despite early optimism, symbolic AI struggled with real-world complexity due to its reliance on predefined rules.

1

This led to the rise of connectionism, a paradigm shift spearheaded by Geoffrey Hinton and his work on artificial neural networks. Deep learning, a subset of connectionist AI, has since revolutionized the field by enabling machines to learn from vast amounts of data through multi-layered neural architectures.

Today, AI encompasses a spectrum of techniques, from traditional rule-based expert systems to advanced generative models capable of producing human-like text, images, and even synthetic personalities. However, at the heart of AI's functionality lies the concept of intelligent agents—autonomous systems designed to perceive their environment and take actions that maximize their success in achieving specific goals.

AI Agents vs. Traditional Software

The distinction between AI agents and conventional software is fundamental to understanding the transformative potential of AI. Traditional software follows predefined instructions, executing tasks in a deterministic manner without adapting to new information beyond its programmed scope. AI agents, on the other hand, exhibit autonomy, learning capabilities, and decision-making processes that allow them to operate in dynamic environments.

An AI agent is defined as any entity that perceives its surroundings through sensors and acts upon that environment through effectors. Unlike static programs, AI agents continuously refine their understanding through interaction and experience. Consider the difference between a conventional email spam filter and an AI-powered cybersecurity agent. A traditional spam filter relies on fixed rules and keyword-based filtering, whereas an AI cybersecurity agent employs machine learning to detect evolving threats, recognize malicious patterns, and adapt in real-time to counter cyberattacks.

AI agents possess the following distinguishing characteristics:

1. **Perception** – AI agents interpret data from their environment, which may include visual inputs, audio signals, or structured information from databases.

2. **Autonomy** – Unlike traditional software, AI agents make decisions and take actions without requiring human intervention.

3. **Learning** – Advanced AI agents employ machine learning to improve their performance over time.

4. **Goal-Driven Behavior** – AI agents optimize their actions based on predefined objectives or reward mechanisms.

5. **Adaptability** – AI agents modify their strategies based on environmental changes, user interactions, or learned experiences.

AI agents serve as the foundation for intelligent systems that power applications ranging from autonomous vehicles to real-time financial trading algorithms. Understanding their architecture and functionality is essential to leveraging AI's full potential.

Types of AI Agents and Their Functions

AI agents are classified based on their design, capabilities, and level of intelligence. The following categories represent the primary types of AI agents in use today:

Reactive Agents

Reactive agents are the simplest form of AI agents. They respond to inputs from their environment based on predefined rules without maintaining an internal representation of past states. These agents are highly efficient for structured tasks but lack long-term learning capabilities.

Example: A chess-playing AI that evaluates possible moves and selects the best one without considering past games or future strategies beyond a predefined depth.

Goal-Based Agents

Goal-based agents operate by assessing potential actions that lead to a defined objective. Unlike reactive agents, these systems maintain an internal model that allows them to evaluate different courses of action before executing decisions.

Example: Autonomous navigation systems in self-driving cars that calculate the optimal route while considering traffic conditions, road safety, and energy efficiency.

Utility-Based Agents

Utility-based agents extend goal-based systems by incorporating a utility function that quantifies the desirability of different outcomes. Instead of merely achieving a goal, these agents prioritize the most efficient, effective, or rewarding solution.

Example: AI-powered recommendation engines that analyze user preferences and suggest personalized content with the highest likelihood of engagement.

Learning Agents

Learning agents possess the ability to improve their performance by analyzing past experiences. They incorporate elements of machine learning, reinforcement learning, and self-supervised learning to refine their decision-making processes.

Example: AI-driven fraud detection systems that adapt to emerging cyber threats by continuously learning from new transaction patterns and anomalies.

These classifications highlight the varying degrees of intelligence and adaptability present in AI systems. By understanding how AI agents function, businesses, researchers, and individuals can harness their potential to drive innovation and efficiency.

Case Study of an AI-Powered Customer Support Agent

To illustrate the capabilities of AI agents in real-world applications, consider the case of an AI-powered customer support agent deployed by a multinational technology firm.

Problem Statement

The company faced increasing customer service demands, resulting in long response times and inconsistent support quality. Traditional chatbot solutions failed to address complex queries, leading to high customer frustration and attrition rates.

AI Implementation

The company integrated a learning-based AI support agent that utilized:

- **Natural Language Processing (NLP)** to understand user queries and extract intent.

- **Reinforcement Learning** to improve responses based on customer satisfaction feedback.

- **Knowledge Graphs** to provide accurate and contextually relevant information.

- **Sentiment Analysis** to detect frustration levels and escalate issues to human agents when necessary.

Outcome and Impact

Within six months, the AI-powered agent achieved:

- **A 40 percent reduction in response times** by streamlining query resolution.

- **A 60 percent increase in customer satisfaction ratings** through more personalized interactions.

- **Operational cost savings exceeding 30 percent** by reducing reliance on human support representatives.

This case study exemplifies how AI agents can enhance efficiency, optimize user experiences, and provide scalable solutions across industries.

Conclusion

AI and intelligent agents represent the next frontier of technological transformation. Unlike traditional software, AI agents exhibit autonomy, learning, and adaptability, allowing them to navigate complex and dynamic environments. By classifying AI agents into reactive, goal-based, utility-based, and learning models, we can better understand their potential applications and limitations.

Real-world implementations, such as AI-powered customer support systems, demonstrate the profound impact of AI agents in industries ranging from finance to healthcare. As AI continues to evolve, understanding its mechanisms and applications will be essential for anyone seeking to remain competitive in the digital age.

The following chapters will explore deeper layers of AI agent architectures, advanced decision-making models, and the ethical considerations surrounding autonomous AI systems. The journey into AI mastery begins with a fundamental comprehension of intelligent agents, but it extends into a realm where AI becomes a collaborative force shaping the future of human progress.

CHAPTER 2
The Building Blocks of AI

Artificial intelligence is not a singular entity but a complex fusion of mathematical theories, computational models, and cognitive principles designed to simulate human-like intelligence. To comprehend AI's full potential, it is essential to dissect its fundamental components: machine learning, deep learning, natural language processing, and reinforcement learning. These core domains represent the mechanisms by which AI systems perceive, analyze, and act upon information.

This chapter explores how AI "thinks" by examining decision-making frameworks, cognitive architectures, and algorithmic logic. It then introduces the three foundational pillars of AI—data, algorithms, and computational power—before addressing the ethical concerns that arise as AI systems grow increasingly autonomous and influential.

By the end of this chapter, the reader will gain a structured, research-backed understanding of the fundamental building blocks that empower AI systems across industries.

Core AI Concepts: Machine Learning, Deep Learning, NLP, and Reinforcement Learning

Machine Learning:

11

Machine learning (ML) is the backbone of artificial intelligence. It enables systems to recognize patterns, make predictions, and optimize decision-making through experience rather than explicit programming. The origins of ML can be traced back to Alan Turing's concept of a "learning machine," later formalized by Arthur Samuel in 1959. Samuel defined machine learning as "the field of study that gives computers the ability to learn without being explicitly programmed."

Machine learning algorithms are categorized into three primary types:

- **Supervised Learning**: The system is trained on labeled data, where input-output mappings are explicitly provided. Examples include image recognition models that classify objects and fraud detection systems in banking.

- **Unsupervised Learning**: The system identifies patterns in unlabeled data, often used in clustering and anomaly detection. Market segmentation and genetic sequence analysis are common applications.

- **Reinforcement Learning**: The system learns through trial and error by interacting with an environment and receiving rewards or penalties. This approach is crucial in robotics, game AI, and autonomous systems.

The development of powerful algorithms such as support vector machines, decision trees, and gradient boosting has accelerated the capabilities of ML in various domains.

Deep Learning:

Deep learning (DL) is a subfield of ML that mimics the structure and function of the human brain through artificial neural networks. Unlike traditional ML models, which rely on feature engineering, deep learning autonomously extracts hierarchical representations from data.

The foundation of deep learning can be traced to the 1943 work of Warren McCulloch and Walter Pitts, who proposed a mathematical model of neurons. However, the true revolution began with Geoffrey Hinton's work on backpropagation and the resurgence of neural networks in the 2000s.

Key architectures in deep learning include:

- **Convolutional Neural Networks (CNNs)**: Specialized for image recognition, used in facial recognition and medical imaging.

- **Recurrent Neural Networks (RNNs)**: Designed for sequential data processing, applied in speech recognition and financial time-series forecasting.

- **Transformers**: The backbone of modern AI language models such as GPT-4 and Google Gemini, enabling unprecedented advances in natural language processing.

Deep learning's ability to analyze vast amounts of unstructured data has revolutionized industries from healthcare to finance, paving the way for advanced autonomous systems.

Natural Language Processing:

Natural language processing (NLP) enables AI to understand, interpret, and generate human language. The history of NLP dates back to early rule-based models and the famous ELIZA chatbot developed by Joseph Weizenbaum in 1966.

Modern NLP relies on statistical and deep learning methods, with key advancements including:

- **Word Embeddings**: Techniques such as Word2Vec and GloVe that represent words in a high-dimensional space, improving semantic understanding.

- **Transformer Models**: Introduced by Vaswani et al. in 2017, transformers have become the dominant architecture for NLP, powering systems such as ChatGPT and BERT.

- **Few-Shot and Zero-Shot Learning**: AI models that generalize across multiple tasks with minimal training data, enhancing adaptability.

NLP underpins real-world applications such as chatbots, machine translation, sentiment analysis, and AI-powered content generation.

Reinforcement Learning:

Reinforcement learning (RL) enables AI systems to learn optimal behaviors through interaction with an environment. Inspired by behavioral psychology, RL employs reward-based learning to develop intelligent agents capable of complex decision-making.

Seminal contributions in RL include:

- **Q-Learning**: A model-free algorithm introduced by Watkins in 1989 that enables agents to learn optimal policies.

- **Deep Q-Networks (DQN)**: A deep learning-based RL approach developed by DeepMind, which allowed AI to master Atari games with human-level performance.

- **AlphaGo**: A groundbreaking RL-based AI that defeated the world champion in the game of Go, demonstrating the power of deep reinforcement learning.

Reinforcement learning is fundamental in autonomous systems, including robotic automation, self-driving cars, and algorithmic trading.

How AI "Thinks" and Processes Information

Artificial intelligence processes information using a combination of probabilistic reasoning, pattern recognition, and optimization techniques. Unlike human cognition, AI decision-making is rooted in mathematical logic and statistical inference.

Symbolic AI vs. Connectionist AI

AI reasoning can be classified into two paradigms:

1. **Symbolic AI (GOFAI - Good Old-Fashioned AI)**: Based on formal logic, rule-based systems, and

knowledge graphs. IBM's Watson and expert systems exemplify this approach.

2. **Connectionist AI**: Rooted in neural networks, connectionist AI learns from data without explicit rules. Modern deep learning models belong to this category.

While symbolic AI excels at structured reasoning, connectionist AI dominates in perception and pattern recognition. Hybrid models are being developed to integrate both approaches.

Bayesian Inference and Probabilistic Reasoning

AI systems leverage probabilistic methods such as Bayesian inference to update beliefs based on new information. Judea Pearl's work on Bayesian networks revolutionized AI decision-making, enabling applications in medical diagnosis, robotics, and cybersecurity.

Markov Decision Processes (MDP)

Markov Decision Processes provide a mathematical framework for sequential decision-making under uncertainty.

Used extensively in RL, MDPs model AI behaviors in complex environments, from autonomous vehicles to financial risk assessment.

The Three Pillars of AI Mastery

1. **Data**: The lifeblood of AI, encompassing structured and unstructured datasets. The success of AI models depends on data quality, diversity, and volume.

2. **Algorithms**: The core logic that enables AI systems to learn, adapt, and optimize decisions. Advanced architectures continue to push the boundaries of AI's capabilities.

3. **Computing Power**: The exponential growth of processing power, fueled by GPUs, TPUs, and quantum computing, is accelerating AI's potential. Cloud-based AI services now provide unprecedented scalability.

The Dark Side of Intelligent Systems

While AI presents immense opportunities, it also raises ethical concerns:

- **Bias and Fairness**: AI systems can inherit biases from training data, leading to discrimination in hiring, lending, and law enforcement.

- **Privacy Risks**: AI-driven surveillance and data collection pose significant threats to individual privacy.

- **Autonomous Decision-Making**: The rise of lethal autonomous weapons and AI-driven financial trading highlights the risks of unchecked AI autonomy.

The development of ethical AI frameworks is crucial to ensuring responsible deployment and mitigating unintended consequences.

Artificial intelligence is an evolving field that integrates machine learning, deep learning, NLP, and reinforcement learning. By understanding how AI processes information and recognizing the foundational pillars of AI—data, algorithms, and computing power—one gains insight into its transformative potential. However, ethical considerations must remain at the forefront as AI continues to shape the future of society.

CHAPTER 3
Getting Started with AI Development

Artificial intelligence development is no longer reserved for research institutions and technology giants. With the rapid evolution of AI tools, frameworks, and cloud-based solutions, developers at all levels can build intelligent systems with unprecedented ease. However, to create AI applications that are both powerful and reliable, one must understand the underlying principles, choose the right tools, and follow best practices for implementation.

This chapter serves as a structured guide for aspiring AI developers. It provides an in-depth examination of programming languages, AI development platforms, and step-by-step instructions for setting up an AI environment. Finally, a hands-on project will solidify these concepts, allowing readers to create their first AI-powered agent.

The AI Developer's Toolkit

AI development requires a well-equipped toolkit that includes programming languages, libraries, and platforms optimized for machine learning and deep learning. Selecting the appropriate language depends on the problem being addressed, the scalability of the solution, and the ease of integration with existing systems.

1. Python

Python dominates AI development due to its simplicity, versatility, and extensive ecosystem. Libraries such as Tensor-Flow, PyTorch, Scikit-learn, and NLTK enable developers to build and deploy models efficiently.

- **TensorFlow**: An open-source machine learning framework developed by Google, offering flexibility for deep learning and AI-powered applications.

- **PyTorch**: A highly popular deep learning framework developed by Facebook, known for its dynamic computation graph and user-friendly interface.

- **Scikit-learn**: Ideal for traditional machine learning tasks such as classification, regression, and clustering.

- **NLTK and spaCy**: Essential for natural language processing (NLP) tasks, such as text classification and named entity recognition.

Python's ecosystem makes it the best choice for both beginners and experts. Its readability and broad support across AI domains ensure that developers can rapidly prototype and deploy models.

2. JavaScript

JavaScript, though not traditionally associated with AI, has become increasingly relevant with the rise of AI-powered web applications. Libraries such as TensorFlow.js allow for in-browser machine learning, enabling developers to run models on the client side without requiring server-side processing.

- **TensorFlow.js**: A JavaScript version of TensorFlow that allows deep learning models to run within web browsers.

- **Brain.js**: A neural network library optimized for JavaScript applications.

- **ConvNetJS**: A deep learning library designed for real-time in-browser applications.

JavaScript is particularly useful for AI-driven user interfaces, interactive web applications, and real-time inference in web browsers.

3. R

R is widely used in statistical computing, data visualization, and predictive modeling. It excels in applications where deep statistical analysis is required.

- **Caret**: A comprehensive package for machine learning in R.

- **ggplot2**: A powerful tool for visualizing AI-generated insights.

- **RandomForest and XGBoost**: Key libraries for decision trees and ensemble learning.

Though R is not the first choice for deep learning, it remains indispensable in research and data-driven AI applications.

4. Other Notable Languages

- **C++**: Used in performance-critical AI applications, such as computer vision and robotics.

- **Java**: A strong choice for large-scale enterprise AI applications.

- **Julia**: A newer language optimized for high-performance numerical computing and AI research.

Choosing the right language depends on the project requirements, scalability considerations, and ease of deployment.

Choosing the Right AI Development Platform

AI development platforms provide pre-built frameworks, APIs, and computational tools that accelerate the model development process. The selection of a platform depends on the complexity of the task, scalability needs, and integration requirements.

1. TensorFlow

TensorFlow provides an end-to-end framework for developing machine learning and deep learning models. Its key features include:

- **Keras API**: A high-level API that simplifies deep learning model development.

- **TensorFlow Lite**: Optimized for deploying AI models on mobile and edge devices,

- **TensorFlow Extended (TFX)**: A production-ready framework for deploying AI in enterprise environments.

TensorFlow is widely used in healthcare, finance, and robotics due to its flexibility and scalability.

2. PyTorch

PyTorch is preferred for academic research and experimental AI projects due to its dynamic computation graph, making it easier to debug and modify models in real-time.

- **TorchScript**: Enables model deployment in production environments.

- **ONNX Support**: Allows interoperability between AI frameworks.

- **Hugging Face Integration**: Supports cutting-edge NLP models such as GPT and BERT.

PyTorch's user-friendly nature and strong support from the AI research community make it an excellent choice for developing innovative models.

3. OpenAI

OpenAI provides advanced APIs and tools for large-scale AI applications, including:

- **GPT (Generative Pre-trained Transformer)**: A state-of-the-art language model for text generation, conversation, and automation.

- **DALL·E**: An AI model for generating images from textual descriptions.

- **Codex**: The engine behind GitHub Copilot, used for AI-assisted programming.

OpenAI tools are ideal for developers looking to integrate advanced NLP, image generation, and AI-driven automation into their applications.

4. LangChain

LangChain is a framework for building AI-driven applications that integrate multiple models, APIs, and real-world interactions. Its use cases include:

- **Conversational AI**: Enables AI models to interact with external data sources.

- **Document Processing**: Enhances AI applications that require real-time document parsing.

- **Autonomous AI Agents**: Facilitates workflow automation and decision-making models.

LangChain is gaining traction in enterprise AI solutions, providing developers with a structured approach to integrating AI models into practical applications.

Setting Up Your First AI Development Environment

To begin AI development, one must set up a structured environment that includes essential libraries and tools.

Step 1: Install Python and Virtual Environment

```
1. sudo apt update && sudo apt install python3 python3-venv python3-pip
2. python3 -m venv ai_env
3. source ai_env/bin/activate
4.
```

Step 2: Install Key AI Libraries

```
1. pip install numpy pandas matplotlib scikit-learn tensorflow torch
2.
```

Step 3: Verify Installation

```
1. import tensorflow as tf
2. import torch
3.
4. print(tf.__version__)
5. print(torch.__version__)
6.
```

This setup ensures that all necessary dependencies are installed and functional.

Creating Your First AI Agent – A Simple Rule-Based Chatbot

Developing an AI chatbot is an excellent first project for understanding fundamental AI logic. This chatbot will respond to user input based on predefined rules.

Step 1: Define Response Rules

```
1. responses = {
2.    "hello": "Hello! How can I assist you?",
3.    "how are you": "I am an AI chatbot, always ready to help!",
4.    "bye": "Goodbye! Have a great day!",
5. }
6.
7. def chatbot_response(user_input):
8.    return responses.get(user_input.lower(), "I do not understand that.")
9.
```

Step 2: Run the Chatbot

```
1. while True:
2.    user_input = input("You: ")
3.    if user_input.lower() == "exit":
4.       break
5.    print("Bot:", chatbot_response(user_input))
6.
```

This basic chatbot provides a foundation for building more sophisticated AI agents using NLP and machine learning techniques.

This chapter provided a structured roadmap for AI development, covering programming languages, platforms, and practical implementation strategies. The mini project introduced the basics of AI-driven conversations, setting the stage for more advanced AI applications.

The next chapter will explore Machine Learning and Neural Networks, where we will delve into model training, optimization, and real-world deployment strategies.

CHAPTER 4
Supervised & Unsupervised Learning

Artificial intelligence thrives on data. It learns patterns, derives insights, and refines its decision-making processes by analyzing vast quantities of structured and unstructured information. At the heart of AI's intelligence lies machine learning, an intricate system of algorithms that empower machines to recognize trends, make predictions, and optimize outcomes.

This chapter explores the two fundamental paradigms of machine learning: supervised learning and unsupervised learning. These approaches define how AI agents process information, refine their models, and generate valuable insights. The chapter will also cover the critical role of feature engineering, a practice that significantly influences the performance of machine learning models. Finally, readers will engage with a hands-on project—building a simple machine learning model—before delving into a real-world case study on AI-powered fraud detection in the banking industry.

How AI Agents Learn from Information

Machine learning operates on a simple principle: learning from data. Unlike traditional programming, where explicit rules define behavior, machine learning allows systems to infer patterns from examples. This ability to generalize from data is what enables AI agents to predict stock prices, detect fraudulent transactions, classify medical images, and generate human-like text.

Supervised learning and **unsupervised** learning represent two contrasting methodologies in how AI learns:

- **Supervised Learning**: The AI agent learns from labeled data, meaning every input is associated with a corresponding correct output. It iteratively adjusts its model until it can reliably predict outcomes for unseen data.

- **Unsupervised Learning**: The AI agent explores unlabeled data, identifying hidden structures and relationships without predefined categories. It excels in clustering, anomaly detection, and pattern recognition.

These two learning approaches drive modern AI applications, from recommendation engines to fraud detection systems. Understanding their differences and applications is essential for AI development.

Supervised Learning

Supervised learning relies on training data that includes both inputs and their correct outputs. The AI system uses this dataset to adjust its parameters until it minimizes the error between predictions and actual outcomes.

Common Supervised Learning Algorithms

1. **Linear Regression**: Used for predicting continuous values, such as stock prices, real estate valuations, and sales forecasting.

2. **Logistic Regression**: Ideal for binary classification problems, including spam detection and medical diagnosis.

3. **Decision Trees**: Used in classification and regression tasks, offering interpretable decision-making processes.

4. **Support Vector Machines (SVMs)**: Powerful in high-dimensional spaces, often applied in **image recognition and bioinformatics**.

5. **Neural Networks**: Fundamental to deep learning, enabling advanced applications such as **self-driving cars, voice recognition, and natural language processing**.

Real-World Applications of Supervised Learning

- **Healthcare**: AI models diagnose diseases by analyzing labeled medical images and patient histories.

- **Finance**: Predictive models assess credit risk, flag fraudulent transactions, and optimize investment strategies.

- **E-commerce**: Recommendation engines suggest products based on past purchases and browsing behavior.

Unsupervised Learning

Unsupervised learning identifies hidden structures in raw data without predefined labels. It is especially valuable when human-labeled data is unavailable or costly to obtain.

Common Unsupervised Learning Techniques

1. **Clustering**: Groups similar data points together, often used in **customer segmentation and anomaly detection**.

   - **K-Means**: A popular clustering algorithm for **market segmentation and image compression**.

- o **Hierarchical Clustering**: Builds tree-like structures to categorize data, useful in **biological taxonomy and document classification**.

2. **Dimensionality Reduction**: Reduces data complexity while preserving meaningful patterns.

   - o **Principal Component Analysis (PCA)**: Used in **image compression, genetics, and financial modeling**.

   - o **t-Distributed Stochastic Neighbor Embedding (t-SNE)**: Visualizes high-dimensional data, often applied in **deep learning model analysis**.

3. **Anomaly Detection**: Identifies unusual data points, critical in **fraud detection and cybersecurity**.

Real-World Applications of Unsupervised Learning

- **Cybersecurity**: AI detects network anomalies indicative of cyberattacks.

- **Retail**: Businesses analyze customer behavior to refine marketing strategies.

- **Healthcare**: Unsupervised learning identifies rare diseases and medical anomalies.

Feature Engineering

Feature engineering is the process of selecting, transforming, and creating variables that enhance a model's performance. Well-engineered features allow AI to **capture meaningful patterns, reduce overfitting, and improve prediction accuracy**.

Feature Engineering Techniques

1. **Scaling & Normalization**: Adjusting data ranges to ensure even weighting in machine learning models.

2. **Encoding Categorical Variables**: Converting text-based data into numerical values using **one-hot encoding** or **label encoding**.

3. **Polynomial Features**: Creating interaction terms to capture complex relationships.

4. **Dimensionality Reduction**: Using PCA or autoencoders to reduce redundant information.

Real-World Impact of Feature Engineering

- **Finance**: Transforming raw transaction data into meaningful risk indicators.

- **Healthcare**: Creating medical risk factors from patient histories.

- **Autonomous Vehicles**: Extracting sensor-derived driving patterns for better navigation.

Building & Training a Simple Machine Learning Model

This section provides a step-by-step walkthrough for implementing a basic supervised learning model using Python and **Scikit-Learn**.

Step 1: Installing Dependencies

```
1. pip install numpy pandas scikit-learn matplotlib seaborn
2.
```

Step 2: Importing Libraries

```
1. import numpy as np
2. import pandas as pd
3. import matplotlib.pyplot as plt
4. import seaborn as sns
5. from sklearn.model_selection import train_test_split
6. from sklearn.linear_model import LinearRegression
7. from sklearn.metrics import mean_squared_error
8.
```

Step 3: Loading and Splitting Data

```
1. data = pd.read_csv('house_prices.csv')
2. X = data[['square_feet', 'bedrooms', 'bathrooms']]
```

```
3. y = data['price']
4. X_train, X_test, y_train, y_test = train_test_split(X, y, test_size=0.2, ran-
dom_state=42)
5.
```

Step 4: Training the Model

```
1. model = LinearRegression()
2. model.fit(X_train, y_train)
3.
```

Step 5: Making Predictions

```
1. predictions = model.predict(X_test)
2. print("Mean Squared Error:", mean_squared_error(y_test, predictions))
3.
```

AI-Powered Fraud Detection in Banking

Fraudulent financial transactions cost billions annually, prompting banks to adopt AI-driven fraud detection systems.

How AI Detects Fraud

1. **Supervised Learning Models**: Classify transactions as fraudulent or legitimate using labeled datasets.

2. **Unsupervised Learning Models**: Identify unusual spending patterns and transaction anomalies.

3. **Hybrid Models**: Combine supervised and unsupervised learning for enhanced accuracy.

Industry Implementation

- **JPMorgan Chase** employs AI to monitor real-time transactions and detect fraud in milliseconds.

- **PayPal** utilizes machine learning to flag suspicious activities and reduce chargeback fraud.

- **Mastercard** integrates AI with blockchain to enhance transaction security.

Supervised and unsupervised learning form the backbone of AI development, powering applications from fraud detection to personalized medicine. Mastering these paradigms, along with feature engineering techniques, allows developers to optimize models for real-world challenges. The next chapter will explore **reinforcement learning and self-supervised learning**, uncovering how AI agents evolve through continuous feedback and adaptation.

CHAPTER 5
Deep Learning for AI Agents

In the relentless pursuit of artificial intelligence, deep learning has emerged as the defining breakthrough that has propelled AI agents from rudimentary rule-based systems to sophisticated, self-learning entities. At the heart of this revolution lies the neural network—an intricate mathematical construct inspired by the human brain. These networks serve as the cognitive foundation of AI agents, enabling them to process vast amounts of data, recognize patterns, and make autonomous decisions with unprecedented accuracy.

To grasp the transformative power of deep learning, one must first understand its origins, theoretical underpinnings, and architectural advancements. This chapter will explore the inner workings of neural networks, tracing their development from early perceptrons to modern deep architectures. We will then embark on a hands-on journey, constructing and training an image recognition AI agent using Tensor-Flow. Finally, we will examine a case study illustrating the life-saving applications of deep learning in medical diagnosis.

The Birth of Neural Networks

The concept of neural networks dates back to the 1940s when Warren McCulloch and Walter Pitts introduced the first mathematical model of an artificial neuron. Their work laid the foundation for perceptrons, a primitive form of neural networks developed by Frank Rosenblatt in 1958. These early networks, while promising, were limited in their ability to solve complex problems. It was not until the 1980s that Geoffrey Hinton, David Rumelhart, and Ronald Williams revolutionized the field with the backpropagation algorithm, enabling multi-layered networks to learn from errors and refine their predictions.

The resurgence of neural networks in the 21st century can be attributed to three key factors:

1. **Computational Advancements** – The exponential growth of processing power, particularly with GPUs and TPUs, has enabled deep networks to train on massive datasets.

2. **Big Data** – The digital era has produced vast repositories of structured and unstructured data, providing neural networks with the fuel they require to learn.

3. **Algorithmic Innovations** – Breakthroughs such as convolutional neural networks (CNNs), recurrent neural networks (RNNs), and transformer architectures have dramatically improved AI's ability to understand images, speech, and language.

From AlphaGo's strategic mastery of board games to OpenAI's GPT models revolutionizing natural language processing, deep learning has reshaped the technological landscape.

The Architecture of Neural Networks

At their core, neural networks are composed of interconnected layers of artificial neurons that process information in a hierarchical manner. Each neuron performs a weighted sum of its inputs, applies an activation function, and propagates the result forward.

A standard feedforward neural network consists of:

1. **Input Layer** – The initial layer that receives raw data, such as pixel values in image processing.

2. **Hidden Layers** – Intermediate layers where complex feature extraction and pattern recognition occur. Deep networks may have dozens or even hundreds of hidden layers.

3. **Output Layer** – The final layer that produces a prediction, classification, or decision.

Activation Functions: Enabling Non-Linearity

To model complex relationships, neural networks rely on activation functions, which introduce non-linearity into the system. Common activation functions include:

- **Sigmoid** – Maps inputs to a range between 0 and 1, useful for probability-based outputs.

- **ReLU (Rectified Linear Unit)** – The most widely used function, enabling efficient training of deep networks by allowing only positive values to propagate.

- **Softmax** – Converts raw outputs into probability distributions for multi-class classification.

Backpropagation and Gradient Descent

Learning in neural networks is achieved through backpropagation, a process that iteratively adjusts the weights of neurons using gradient descent. This optimization technique minimizes the error between predicted and actual outputs by computing partial derivatives of the loss function.

Mathematically, gradient descent updates weights as follows:

$$W := W - \alpha \frac{\partial L}{\partial W}$$

where W represents weights, α\alphaα is the learning rate, and ∂L/W∂ is the gradient of the loss function.

The choice of optimization algorithm significantly influences training efficiency. Popular approaches include:

- **Stochastic Gradient Descent (SGD)** – Updates weights after processing each training example.

- **Adam Optimizer** – A momentum-based variant that adapts learning rates dynamically.

Building a Neural Network from Scratch

Before leveraging high-level libraries like TensorFlow, understanding the fundamental construction of a neural network is essential. Below is a Python implementation of a simple feedforward network using NumPy.

Step 1: Import Dependencies

```
1. import numpy as np
2.
3. # Activation function (ReLU)
4. def relu(x):
5.     return np.maximum(0, x)
6.
```

```
7. # Derivative of ReLU for backpropagation
8. def relu_derivative(x):
9.     return np.where(x > 0, 1, 0)
10.
```

Step 2: Initialize Network Parameters

```
1. np.random.seed(42)
2. input_size = 3
3. hidden_size = 4
4. output_size = 1
5.
6. # Random weight initialization
7. W1 = np.random.randn(input_size, hidden_size)
8. W2 = np.random.randn(hidden_size, output_size)
9.
```

Step 3: Forward and Backpropagation

```
1. def forward(x):
2.     hidden = relu(np.dot(x, W1))
3.     output = np.dot(hidden, W2)
4.     return output, hidden
5.
6. def backward(x, y, output, hidden, learning_rate=0.01):
7.     error = y - output
8.     dW2 = np.dot(hidden.T, error)
9.     dW1 = np.dot(x.T, np.dot(error, W2.T) * relu_derivative(hidden))
10.
11.     global W1, W2
12.     W1 += learning_rate * dW1
13.     W2 += learning_rate * dW2
14.
15.
```

This foundational implementation provides an intuitive grasp of neural network mechanics. Next, we will apply TensorFlow to train an AI agent for image recognition.

Training an Image Recognition AI Agent with TensorFlow

Dataset and Model Setup

We will train a convolutional neural network (CNN) on the MNIST dataset, a collection of handwritten digits.

```
1. import tensorflow as tf
2. from tensorflow.keras import layers, models
3.
4. # Load dataset
5. mnist = tf.keras.datasets.mnist
6. (x_train, y_train), (x_test, y_test) = mnist.load_data()
7. x_train, x_test = x_train / 255.0, x_test / 255.0  # Normalize
8.
9. # Define CNN model
10. model = models.Sequential([
11.    layers.Conv2D(32, (3,3), activation='relu', input_shape=(28, 28, 1)),
12.    layers.MaxPooling2D((2,2)),
13.    layers.Flatten(),
14.    layers.Dense(128, activation='relu'),
15.    layers.Dense(10, activation='softmax')
16. ])
17.
18. # Compile and train
19.    model.compile(optimizer='adam', loss='sparse_categorical_crossentropy', metrics=['accuracy'])
```

```
20. model.fit(x_train, y_train, epochs=5, validation_data=(x_test, y_test))
21.
22.
```

This model effectively classifies handwritten digits with high accuracy.

How Deep Learning is Used in Medical Diagnosis

Deep learning has revolutionized medical diagnostics, particularly in radiology. AI-driven image analysis has achieved expert-level accuracy in detecting conditions such as pneumonia, cancer, and diabetic retinopathy.

AI-Powered Cancer Detection

A study by Stanford University demonstrated that convolutional neural networks could diagnose skin cancer with accuracy comparable to dermatologists. By training on over 100,000 images, the AI system learned to identify malignant lesions with remarkable precision. Such advancements hold the potential to democratize healthcare, enabling early detection in underserved regions.

Deep learning represents the pinnacle of modern AI, transforming fields as diverse as finance, robotics, and medicine. As neural networks continue to evolve, their capabilities will surpass current limitations, ushering in a new era of intelligent AI agents. This chapter has provided both theoretical insights and hands-on applications, equipping readers with the knowledge to explore the limitless potential of deep learning.

CHAPTER 6
Reinforcement Learning for AI Agents

A child learning to walk stumbles countless times before taking their first confident steps. A chess grandmaster internalizes patterns through thousands of games, refining their strategy with every move. Intelligence, in both biological and artificial forms, emerges from experience. Reinforcement learning (RL) is the computational manifestation of this process. It enables AI agents to navigate uncertainty, optimize decisions, and improve performance through repeated interactions with an environment.

This chapter explores reinforcement learning as a cornerstone of artificial intelligence, tracing its theoretical foundations, computational models, and groundbreaking real-world applications. From Markov decision processes to Q-learning and deep reinforcement learning, we will examine how machines learn through rewards and penalties. Finally, we will construct a reinforcement learning agent and analyze case studies where AI has surpassed human expertise in games like Chess, Go, and Starcraft.

The Mathematics of Learning from Interaction

Reinforcement learning is inspired by behavioral psychology, particularly the principles of operant conditioning established by B. F. Skinner. In AI, reinforcement learning formalizes this concept into a computational framework where an agent interacts with an environment, receives feedback in the form of rewards or penalties, and adjusts its actions to maximize cumulative rewards over time.

At its core, reinforcement learning is defined by five key components:

1. **Agent** – The entity that makes decisions.

2. **Environment** – The world in which the agent operates.

3. **State (S)** – The current situation of the agent within the environment.

4. **Action (A)** – The choices available to the agent.

5. **Reward (R)** – A numerical signal indicating the immediate benefit or cost of an action.

The agent learns by exploring different actions, receiving feedback, and refining its decision-making policy to maximize long-term rewards.

Markov Decision Processes (MDPs): Reinforcement learning is mathematically framed as a Markov Decision Process (MDP), a fundamental model used to describe decision-making in stochastic environments. An MDP consists of:

- **A set of states (S)**
- **A set of actions (A)**
- **A transition function (T) that maps (S, A) → S'**
- **A reward function (R) that assigns a numerical value to each transition**
- **A discount factor (γ) that determines the importance of future rewards**

The Markov property states that the future state of the environment depends only on the present state and action, not on past states. This assumption simplifies the learning process and allows for tractable solutions.

MDPs provide the theoretical foundation for most reinforcement learning algorithms, including Q-learning and deep reinforcement learning, which enable agents to optimize their strategies in complex environments.

Teaching AI to Make Optimal Decisions

One of the most widely used reinforcement learning algorithms is **Q-learning**, developed by Chris Watkins in 1989. It is a model-free, off-policy algorithm that enables agents to learn optimal action-selection policies through trial and error.

The algorithm is based on the **Q-value function (Q(s, a))**, which estimates the expected cumulative reward for taking action **a** in state **s** and following the optimal policy thereafter. The agent updates the Q-values iteratively using the Bellman equation:

$$Q(s,a) = Q(s,a) + \alpha[R + \gamma \max Q(s',a') - Q(s,a)]$$

Where:

- α **(alpha)** is the learning rate.
- γ **(gamma)** is the discount factor.
- **R** is the immediate reward.
- **s'** is the new state after taking action **a**.

Through repeated exploration and exploitation, Q-learning converges to an optimal policy, guiding the agent toward maximizing long-term rewards.

Deep Reinforcement Learning: Traditional Q-learning struggles in environments with high-dimensional state spaces. Deep reinforcement learning (DRL) addresses this limitation by integrating reinforcement learning with deep neural networks.

Deep Q-Networks (DQN), introduced by DeepMind in 2015, were the first major breakthrough in DRL. Instead of storing Q-values in a table, DQN uses a convolutional neural network to approximate Q-values, allowing it to handle complex environments like video games.

Key innovations in deep reinforcement learning:

- **Experience Replay** – Storing past experiences and replaying them to break correlation between consecutive experiences.
- **Target Networks** – Using a separate target network to stabilize learning.
- **Policy Gradient Methods** – Directly optimizing policies rather than estimating Q-values.

These techniques have enabled AI to achieve human-level or superhuman performance in various tasks, from playing Atari games to controlling robotic arms.

Building an AI Agent to Play Games Using Reinforcement
Learning

To illustrate reinforcement learning in action, we will build a simple AI agent that learns to play a game using Q-learning. We will use Python and OpenAI Gym, a popular reinforcement learning framework.

Step 1: Install Dependencies

Ensure you have Python, OpenAI Gym, and NumPy installed.

```
1. pip install gym numpy
2.
```

Step 2: Create the Environment

We will use the FrozenLake environment, where the agent must navigate a grid to reach a goal while avoiding hazards.

```
1. import gym
2. import numpy as np
3.
4. env = gym.make("FrozenLake-v1", is_slippery=False)
5.
6.
```

Step 3: Initialize the Q-Table

```
1. Q = np.zeros([env.observation_space.n, env.action_space.n])
2. alpha = 0.1   # Learning rate
3. gamma = 0.99  # Discount factor
4. epsilon = 0.1 # Exploration rate
```

5.

Step 4: Train the Agent

```
1. for episode in range(1000):
2.    state = env.reset()[0]
3.    done = False
4.
5.    while not done:
6.        if np.random.rand() < epsilon:
7.            action = env.action_space.sample()  # Explore
8.        else:
9.            action = np.argmax(Q[state])  # Exploit
10.
11.        next_state, reward, done, _, _ = env.step(action)
12.            Q[state, action] = Q[state, action] + alpha * (reward + gamma * np.max(Q[next_state]) - Q[state, action])
13.        state = next_state
14.
15.
```

Step 5: Test the Trained Agent

```
1. state = env.reset()[0]
2. done = False
3.
4. while not done:
5.    action = np.argmax(Q[state])
6.    state, _, done, _, _ = env.step(action)
7.    env.render()
8.
```

Through repeated trials, the AI agent learns an optimal policy to navigate the environment successfully.

AI Beating Humans in Chess, Go, and Starcraft

Reinforcement learning has produced some of the most significant milestones in artificial intelligence.

1. **AlphaGo (2016)** – Developed by DeepMind, AlphaGo used deep reinforcement learning to defeat the world champion Go player Lee Sedol. Unlike traditional game AI, AlphaGo learned strategies through self-play, reaching superhuman proficiency.

2. **AlphaZero (2017)** – An evolution of AlphaGo, AlphaZero learned to master Chess, Shogi, and Go from scratch, without human data, surpassing the strongest human and AI opponents.

3. **OpenAI Five (2018-2019)** – A reinforcement learning-based AI that trained for over 45,000 years in simulated time to defeat human professionals in the game Dota 2.

4. **AlphaStar (2019)** – The first AI to reach Grandmaster level in Starcraft II, demonstrating strategic adaptability, multi-agent collaboration, and long-term planning.

These breakthroughs showcase reinforcement learning's potential to solve complex problems, revolutionizing fields beyond gaming, including robotics, finance, and healthcare.

The Future of Reinforcement Learning

Reinforcement learning represents a fundamental shift in AI, moving beyond static rule-based systems to adaptive, experience-driven intelligence. As research advances, reinforcement learning will unlock unprecedented capabilities, from self-improving robots to autonomous decision-making agents in finance, medicine, and space exploration.

Understanding reinforcement learning is essential for anyone seeking to navigate the future of AI, where learning from experience defines the intelligence of tomorrow.

CHAPTER 7
How AI Understands Language

Language is the foundation of human intelligence, a vast and intricate system that encodes thoughts, emotions, and reasoning into structured patterns of words. Teaching machines to understand and process language has been one of artificial intelligence's greatest challenges, requiring the convergence of linguistics, cognitive science, and computational algorithms.

The journey of Natural Language Processing (NLP) began in the 1950s when Alan Turing proposed the idea of machine intelligence in his seminal paper *Computing Machinery and Intelligence.* Early NLP systems relied on rule-based approaches, in which linguists and computer scientists manually crafted grammatical structures and lexicons for language processing.

In the 1960s, Joseph Weizenbaum's ELIZA demonstrated the first conversational AI. Although it relied on simple pattern-matching rules rather than true understanding, it exposed both the potential and the limitations of early NLP. The 1970s and 1980s saw the emergence of symbolic AI, where systems such as SHRDLU could perform logical reasoning in restricted linguistic environments. However, these early models struggled with the ambiguity and contextual complexity of human language.

The paradigm shifted in the 1990s with the advent of statistical NLP. Researchers moved away from rigid rule-based programming and instead trained models on vast amounts of linguistic data. Hidden Markov Models (HMMs), Naïve Bayes classifiers, and later, support vector machines became instrumental in tasks such as speech recognition, part-of-speech tagging, and named entity recognition.

By the 2010s, deep learning revolutionized NLP. Geoffrey Hinton's breakthroughs in neural networks led to models that could automatically learn representations of text. The introduction of word embeddings, particularly Word2Vec and GloVe, allowed AI to capture semantic meaning beyond simple word frequency. In 2018, Google introduced the Transformer model architecture in *Attention Is All You Need*, leading to the development of powerful Large Language Models (LLMs) such as BERT, GPT, and T5. These models, trained on billions of words, demonstrated an unprecedented ability to generate coherent text, answer questions, and even engage in reasoning.

Today, NLP continues to evolve with reinforcement learning, self-supervised learning, and emergent behaviors in language models. Researchers now explore how AI can develop deeper semantic understanding, navigate linguistic ambiguity, and align with human values.

Tokenization, Stemming, Lemmatization & Other NLP Fundamentals

Before an AI system can analyze text, it must first transform human language into a structured form that machines can process. This transformation begins with fundamental NLP techniques, each playing a crucial role in language comprehension.

Tokenization

Tokenization is the process of breaking text into individual units, known as tokens. These tokens can be words, subwords, or even characters, depending on the granularity required.

For example, consider the sentence:

"Artificial intelligence is transforming industries worldwide."

A simple word-based tokenization might produce:

["Artificial", "intelligence", "is", "transforming", "indus-tries", "worldwide", "."]

However, advanced tokenization methods, such as Byte Pair Encoding (BPE), allow AI to handle out-of-vocabulary words by breaking them into subword units. This enables models like GPT to generate and understand words not explicitly seen during training.

Stemming and Lemmatization

Both stemming and lemmatization reduce words to their base form, which helps models generalize across variations of the same word.

- **Stemming** uses heuristic rules to strip suffixes, often producing non-dictionary words.

    o Example: *running → run, flies → fli*

- **Lemmatization** relies on linguistic analysis to map words to their proper root forms.

    o Example: *running → run, flies → fly*

While stemming is computationally faster, lemmatization provides greater accuracy in understanding context.

Part-of-Speech (POS) Tagging

POS tagging assigns grammatical labels to words, allowing AI to understand sentence structure. For example:

*"She **runs** fast."*

- *Runs* is a **verb** in this sentence.

*"The **runs** were exhilarating."*

- *Runs* is a **noun** in this sentence.

By identifying parts of speech, NLP models improve syntactic parsing, translation, and text generation.

Named Entity Recognition (NER)

NER identifies proper nouns and categorizes them into predefined classes, such as persons, organizations, and locations.

Example:

"Elon Musk founded SpaceX in California."

NER tags:

- *Elon Musk* → **Person**
- *SpaceX* → **Organization**
- *California* → **Location**

NER is widely used in applications such as search engines, chatbots, and financial market analysis.

Sentiment Analysis & Text Classification with AI

Sentiment analysis enables AI to determine the emotional tone of text, classifying opinions as positive, neutral, or negative. This is particularly useful in analyzing product reviews, customer feedback, and social media discussions.

Early sentiment analysis relied on lexicon-based approaches, where predefined dictionaries of positive and negative words guided classification. However, these methods struggled with context, sarcasm, and nuanced expressions.

Today's AI-driven sentiment analysis employs deep learning models, such as recurrent neural networks (RNNs) and transformers, to capture context and sentiment shifts within a sentence.

Consider the sentence:

"I loved the product, but the customer service was terrible."

A rule-based model might misclassify this as positive due to the word *loved*. In contrast, modern AI models can distinguish the mixed sentiment and classify the review appropriately.

Text Classification: Organizing the Digital World

Text classification assigns labels to text data based on its content. It powers spam filters, topic detection in news articles, and content moderation on social media platforms.

Deep learning models such as BERT and RoBERTa enhance text classification by analyzing entire sentences rather than individual words, ensuring higher accuracy.

How AI Analyzes Social Media Sentiment

Social media is a vast ecosystem where millions of opinions are shared daily. Businesses, governments, and financial institutions use AI-powered sentiment analysis to monitor public perception, detect trends, and respond to crises.

During the COVID-19 pandemic, AI-driven sentiment analysis helped governments assess public sentiment toward health policies, vaccine hesitancy, and misinformation.

Financial markets also leverage AI for sentiment analysis. Hedge funds analyze Twitter sentiment to predict stock movements. A positive surge in tweets about a company can signal potential growth, while negative sentiment may indicate declining investor confidence.

Training an AI for Sentiment Analysis

A sentiment analysis model typically follows these steps:

- **Data Collection** – Gather labeled datasets from social media, news sources, or customer reviews.

- **Preprocessing** – Perform tokenization, stop-word removal, and lemmatization to clean the data.

- **Model Selection** – Use pre-trained transformers such as BERT or fine-tune them on specific sentiment datasets.

- **Training & Evaluation** – Train the model on labeled data and validate its accuracy on unseen text.

- **Deployment** – Integrate the model into applications for real-time analysis and decision-making.

The Future of NLP and AI Language Understanding

The progress in NLP has transformed AI from simple rule-based systems to powerful deep learning models that can generate, comprehend, and even reason with language. However, challenges remain. AI still struggles with common sense reasoning, contextual ambiguity, and ethical concerns surrounding bias in language models.

Future advancements in NLP will focus on making AI more explainable, reducing biases, and improving its ability to understand nuance and sarcasm. The ultimate goal is to create AI that not only processes language but also truly understands human intent, emotions, and reasoning.

The journey of AI in language understanding has only just begun.

CHAPTER 8
Building Conversational AI Agents

Conversational AI represents one of the most compelling frontiers in artificial intelligence, where natural language processing (NLP), deep learning, and human-computer interaction converge to create systems capable of engaging in meaningful dialogue. From the earliest rule-based chatbots to the modern era of transformer-based models, the trajectory of conversational AI reflects significant advances in computational linguistics, neural architectures, and machine learning.

Alan Turing's 1950 paper *Computing Machinery and Intelligence* posed the fundamental question, "Can machines think?" This inquiry led to the Turing Test, a foundational concept that continues to shape the design of intelligent agents. ELIZA, developed by Joseph Weizenbaum in 1966, marked one of the first attempts at simulating human-like conversations through pattern-matching techniques. However, it was Geoffrey Hinton's breakthrough in deep learning, coupled with advancements in attention mechanisms introduced by Vaswani et al. in *Attention Is All You Need* (2017), that enabled the rise of large-scale language models capable of context-aware, nuanced conversations.

This chapter explores the core principles of conversational AI, providing a structured framework for understanding how modern chatbot systems process language, generate responses, and adapt to user intent. Additionally, a hands-on guide will walk through building a conversational AI system using state-of-the-art transformer models.

What Makes a Great Chatbot

A successful conversational AI agent must exhibit three fundamental characteristics: context awareness, intent recognition, and high-quality response generation. These attributes differentiate rudimentary chatbots from sophisticated AI-driven virtual assistants.

Context Awareness in Conversational AI

Human conversations are inherently contextual. A well-designed chatbot must track prior exchanges, infer meaning from the dialogue history, and adapt responses accordingly. Early conversational systems lacked memory, responding to each user input in isolation. Modern AI models, particularly those based on recurrent neural networks (RNNs), transformers, and memory-augmented architectures, can maintain long-range dependencies, ensuring continuity in conversations.

The introduction of attention mechanisms has further enhanced context retention. Unlike traditional sequential models, transformers employ self-attention layers to weigh the importance of each token in an input sequence, enabling chatbots to process information holistically rather than sequentially. This advancement allows AI agents to resolve coreference ambiguities, such as distinguishing between multiple subjects in a conversation:

Example:

- User: *John told Mike he was wrong.*

- AI: *Who was wrong—John or Mike?*

A chatbot with limited context awareness may default to random selection, whereas an advanced system can resolve ambiguity by analyzing prior dialogue turns.

Intent Recognition and Natural Language Understanding (NLU)

Conversational AI relies on **natural language understanding (NLU)** to decipher user intent. Intent classification models, trained on vast corpora of human interactions, enable AI agents to categorize inputs into predefined intent labels such as:

- **Informational queries** (*What is the weather like today?*)

- **Transactional requests** (*Book a flight to New York.*)

- **Conversational context maintenance** (*Tell me more about that topic.*)

Traditional intent recognition relied on **n-gram models** and **word embeddings** (Word2Vec, GloVe), but modern approaches leverage **pre-trained transformers** such as **BERT, RoBERTa, and GPT** to capture deep semantic relationships. By analyzing embeddings in high-dimensional vector space, AI agents can infer user intent with remarkable accuracy.

Response Generation: Rule-Based vs. Neural Approaches

Chatbot response generation methods fall into two categories:

1. **Rule-Based Systems:** These systems rely on predefined scripts and decision trees. Though effective for customer service applications, they lack flexibility and struggle with unstructured input.

2. **Neural Conversational Models:** These models generate responses dynamically using deep learning techniques. Generative models such as **GPT-4** fine-tune responses based on conversation history, producing human-like dialogue.

Early AI systems employed **template-based generation**, substituting placeholders within predefined sentence structures. However, neural networks now enable **contextual word generation**, producing responses with grammatical coherence and semantic depth.

Example:

- **Rule-Based Model:** *Hello, how can I assist you today?*
- **Neural Model (GPT-4):** *Good afternoon! How can I help you with your request today?*

Neural models exhibit greater linguistic diversity, making conversations more natural and engaging.

Building a Conversational AI with GPT Models

This section provides a step-by-step guide for developing a conversational AI system using **OpenAI's GPT models**.

1 Setting Up the Development Environment

To begin, ensure that you have Python installed along with the necessary libraries:

```
1. pip install openai transformers flask
2.
```

2 API Integration and Querying GPT Models

The following Python script demonstrates how to query a GPT model for conversational AI:

```
1. import openai
2.
3. openai.api_key = "your_api_key"
4.
5. def chatbot_response(prompt):
6.    response = openai.ChatCompletion.create(
7.        model="gpt-4",
8.        messages=[{"role": "user", "content": prompt}]
9.    )
10.    return response["choices"][0]["message"]["content"]
11.
12. while True:
13.    user_input = input("You: ")
14.    if user_input.lower() == "exit":
15.        break
16.    print("AI:", chatbot_response(user_input))
17.
```

This script enables users to interact with GPT-based chatbots in real time.

Enhancing Your AI Agent with Memory and Context Awareness

A major limitation of traditional chatbots is their inability to retain long-term context. To address this, developers implement **session-based memory**, storing previous interactions to improve response coherence.

Implementing Context Memory

Using a **context window**, we can maintain conversation history across multiple exchanges:

```
1. conversation_history = []
2.
3. def chatbot_response(prompt):
4.     global conversation_history
5.     conversation_history.append({"role": "user", "content": prompt})
6.
7.     response = openai.ChatCompletion.create(
8.         model="gpt-4",
9.         messages=conversation_history
10.    )
11.
12.    assistant_message = response["choices"][0]["message"]["content"]
13.        conversation_history.append({"role": "assistant", "content": assistant_message})
14.
15.    return assistant_message
16.
17.
```

By storing previous exchanges in a structured format, AI agents deliver responses that feel personalized and consistent.

The Rise of AI Virtual Assistants (Siri, Alexa, ChatGPT)

AI-powered virtual assistants have transitioned from simple command-execution tools to sophisticated conversational agents. Apple's **Siri**, Amazon's **Alexa**, and OpenAI's **ChatGPT** exemplify the increasing complexity of AI-driven interactions.

- **Siri (2011):** Rule-based natural language processing, limited contextual awareness.
- **Alexa (2014):** Expanded voice recognition, third-party skill integration.
- **ChatGPT (2023-Present):** Transformer-based architecture with memory retention, multimodal capabilities.

Each advancement reflects deeper levels of **context understanding, intent classification, and response generation**, transforming AI assistants into indispensable tools.

Conclusion: The Future of Conversational AI

The trajectory of conversational AI suggests a future where multimodal AI agents—capable of processing text, voice, and visual data—become seamlessly integrated into daily life. Research into self-supervised learning, reinforcement learning with human feedback (RLHF), and hierarchical memory architectures continues to push the boundaries of AI-driven conversation.

Building intelligent chatbots requires not only technical expertise but also an understanding of cognitive psychology, human linguistic behavior, and computational efficiency. By synthesizing cutting-edge AI advancements with practical applications, conversational AI systems will redefine human-machine interaction for decades to come.

CHAPTER 9
Advanced AI Agent Communication

The ability of artificial intelligence to engage in human-like conversations represents one of the most complex and fascinating challenges in the field of AI. From early rule-based chatbots such as ELIZA, which relied on pattern matching, to modern transformer-based architectures like GPT-4, AI's ability to understand, generate, and retain conversational context has advanced significantly. However, despite these leaps, fundamental challenges remain, including the need for deeper contextual awareness, emotional intelligence, and adaptive learning.

This chapter will explore the mechanisms that enable AI agents to engage in advanced communication. It will examine fine-tuning methodologies for optimizing AI models for specific tasks, analyze the psychological underpinnings of human-AI interactions, and provide a detailed breakdown of multi-turn conversations and context retention. Finally, the chapter will present a step-by-step approach to developing AI agents with distinct personalities and emotional intelligence, ensuring more meaningful and engaging user experiences.

Fine-Tuning Language Models for Specific Tasks

Pretrained language models, such as OpenAI's GPT series and Google's Gemini, serve as the foundation for many conversational AI agents. These models are trained on vast datasets, allowing them to generate human-like text based on statistical probabilities. However, to create AI agents specialized for particular industries or applications, additional fine-tuning is required.

Fine-tuning involves further training a model on a domain-specific dataset to enhance its performance in a particular field. For example, a medical AI assistant would require exposure to medical literature, clinical guidelines, and diagnostic conversations to provide accurate and reliable responses. Similarly, an AI legal assistant must be trained on case law, legal statutes, and contract analysis.

Techniques for Effective Fine-Tuning

1. **Supervised Fine-Tuning**

   - Involves training the model on labeled datasets where correct responses are provided.
   - Ensures accuracy and domain-specific knowledge adaptation.

- Example: A customer support AI trained on historical customer interactions.

2. **Reinforcement Learning from Human Feedback (RLHF)**

   - Utilizes reinforcement learning where human evaluators provide feedback on generated responses.
   - Enhances alignment with human values, tone, and appropriateness.
   - Example: ChatGPT's refinement process, which integrates user feedback to improve responses.

3. **Transfer Learning with Task-Specific Datasets**

   - Leverages a pretrained model's existing linguistic capabilities while adapting it to a new domain.
   - Reduces the need for training from scratch, saving computational resources.
   - Example: A financial AI assistant fine-tuned using market reports and trading analyses.

4. **Prompt Engineering for Task Optimization**

- Uses carefully designed prompts to guide AI behavior without requiring retraining.
- Provides control over response generation and task execution.
- Example: Legal AI prompting strategies that frame responses in a structured legal format.

By implementing these fine-tuning techniques, developers can create AI agents that not only understand general language patterns but also demonstrate domain expertise, enhancing their credibility and reliability in professional settings.

The Psychology of Human-AI Conversations

Human conversations are driven by complex cognitive processes, including memory recall, contextual inference, and emotional engagement. AI models attempting to replicate these interactions must account for several psychological factors:

1. **Theory of Mind in AI**

   - Human communication involves understanding others' beliefs, intentions, and emotions.

- While AI lacks true cognitive awareness, advanced models can approximate user intent through sentiment analysis and behavioral pattern recognition.

2. **Cognitive Load and Information Processing**

   - Users expect AI responses to be concise yet informative.
   - Overloading users with excessive data can reduce engagement, making information prioritization essential.

3. **Trust and the Illusion of Intelligence**

   - Users tend to anthropomorphize AI, attributing human-like qualities to machine responses.
   - This psychological tendency must be managed carefully to prevent over-reliance on AI-generated content in critical decision-making.

4. **Framing Effect and Response Perception**

   - The way an AI response is structured influences user perception.

- Example: Rewording an AI-generated diagnosis can shift a patient's emotional response from fear to reassurance.

Understanding these cognitive principles allows developers to design AI agents that communicate more effectively, ensuring clarity, trustworthiness, and psychological alignment with human conversational patterns.

Multi-Turn Conversations and Context Retention

Many AI models struggle with maintaining conversational continuity across multiple interactions. Key issues include:

- **Token Limitations** – Most language models have constraints on the number of tokens they can process, leading to loss of context in extended conversations.
- **State Management** – AI models often fail to recall past user interactions, requiring additional memory mechanisms.
- **Ambiguity Resolution** – Contextual shifts within a conversation can lead to misinterpretations if prior messages are not correctly referenced.

1. **Memory Augmentation through Vector Databases**

   - AI agents can store past interactions in a vector database, allowing them to retrieve relevant historical context.
   - Example: A customer service AI that remembers a user's previous complaints and adapts responses accordingly.

2. **Hierarchical Attention Mechanisms**

   - Implementing hierarchical attention layers helps models focus on critical context while ignoring irrelevant details.
   - Example: An AI tutor that recalls prior student mistakes and adapts lesson plans dynamically.

3. **Session Persistence and Identity Tracking**

   o Assigning unique user identifiers allows AI models to maintain session continuity across multiple conversations.

- o Example: A financial AI assistant that remembers past investment preferences.

By addressing these challenges, AI agents can provide more fluid and coherent multi-turn conversations, significantly improving user experience and interaction quality.

Building an AI Agent with Personality and Emotional Intelligence

A sterile, mechanical AI can feel impersonal and unengaging. By integrating personality traits and emotional intelligence, AI agents can foster deeper user engagement.

Methods for Developing Personality in AI

1. **Linguistic Style Adaptation**

   - Modifying sentence structure, word choice, and tone to reflect distinct personality traits.
   - Example: A humorous AI assistant using witty remarks versus a formal AI maintaining professionalism.

2. **Emotion Recognition and Sentiment Analysis**

- Implementing natural language processing techniques to detect user emotions.
- Example: A mental health AI that adjusts its tone based on user distress signals.

3. **Behavioral Consistency Models**

- Ensuring AI maintains a consistent personality across different conversations.
- Example: A storytelling AI that maintains a playful and imaginative tone throughout a narrative.

4. **Adaptive Learning from User Preferences**

- Allowing AI to adjust its responses based on repeated interactions.
- Example: A personal AI assistant that learns preferred greeting styles and communication patterns.

By integrating personality and emotional intelligence, AI agents can move beyond transactional interactions, creating a more engaging, human-like experience.

The Future of AI Conversation

Conversational AI has evolved from rudimentary chatbots to sophisticated agents capable of maintaining context, recognizing sentiment, and adapting personality traits. However, the journey is far from complete. The next frontier will involve integrating deeper reasoning abilities, ethical considerations, and multimodal interaction capabilities.

By fine-tuning AI for specific tasks, incorporating cognitive psychology principles, enhancing memory and context retention, and embedding emotional intelligence, developers can create truly advanced AI communication agents. These innovations will define the next era of human-AI interaction, bringing us closer to a world where AI is not just a tool but a compelling conversational partner.

CHAPTER 10
AI Agents That Think & Act

Artificial intelligence has advanced beyond rule-based automation, now emulating cognitive processes that once defined human intelligence. AI agents, designed to think, adapt, and act within dynamic environments, leverage cognitive architectures that integrate perception, decision-making, and action execution. This chapter explores the theoretical underpinnings of AI cognition, the role of computational models in simulating intelligence, and real-world implementations in robotics and automation.

The Evolution of AI Cognitive Architectures

The quest for artificial cognition can be traced to the earliest debates in cognitive science and computer science. Alan Turing's concept of the **Universal Machine** proposed that intelligence could be mechanized through symbolic manipulation. Later, Marvin Minsky and Seymour Papert pioneered **symbolic AI**, or GOFAI (Good Old-Fashioned AI), which sought to represent knowledge through explicit rules and structured data.

The limitations of symbolic AI, particularly in dealing with ambiguity and learning, led to the rise of **connectionism**, which sought to mimic human cognition through artificial neural networks. Geoffrey Hinton's backpropagation algorithm in the 1980s enabled neural networks to learn from data, laying the foundation for modern deep learning.

The shift from handcrafted rule-based systems to self-learning models marked a turning point in AI cognition. Today, cognitive architectures blend symbolic reasoning, neural computation, and probabilistic modeling to create intelligent agents capable of autonomous decision-making.

Key Cognitive Models in AI Agents

To understand how AI agents perceive and act, we must explore the dominant cognitive frameworks guiding their design.

Symbolic AI and Knowledge Representation

Symbolic AI represents intelligence as **explicit symbols** and logical rules. **SOAR** and **ACT-R** are two seminal architectures that structure cognition through **goal-driven reasoning** and **memory-based learning**. These models are well-suited for applications requiring structured knowledge, such as **expert systems** and **strategic decision-making AI**.

Subsymbolic AI and Neural Networks

In contrast, subsymbolic AI does not rely on explicit rules but rather on **statistical learning**. Deep neural networks, modeled after biological neurons, enable AI agents to **recognize patterns, predict outcomes, and optimize decisions**. Reinforcement learning further enhances these agents by allowing them to **learn through trial and error**, refining strategies based on reward functions.

Hybrid Cognitive Architectures

Modern AI systems combine symbolic reasoning with sub-symbolic learning to achieve greater adaptability and explainability. Neurosymbolic AI, championed by researchers such as Yann LeCun, seeks to integrate logical reasoning with neural computation, making AI both interpretable and capable of generalization.

These cognitive architectures form the backbone of intelligent AI agents, enabling them to perceive their environment, process information, and make decisions with increasing autonomy.

How AI Agents Perceive the World

Perception is fundamental to intelligence. AI agents gather data through **sensors, cameras, microphones, and digital inputs**, processing it through various perception models:

- **Computer Vision**: Enables agents to recognize objects, interpret visual scenes, and navigate environments using **convolutional neural networks (CNNs)**.
- **Natural Language Processing (NLP)**: Allows agents to understand and generate human language, utilizing models such as **transformers and self-supervised learning**.
- **Sensor Fusion**: Integrates multiple data streams, such as **LIDAR, sonar, and infrared imaging**, to construct a coherent model of the world.

Once perceived, this information must be transformed into actionable insights, bridging the gap between raw data and intelligent behavior.

Decision-Making in AI Agents

AI decision-making spans from **rule-based logic** to **adaptive learning models**. Key approaches include:

Rule-Based Decision Systems

Early AI relied on if-then logic to dictate actions. While effective in controlled environments, these systems struggle with uncertainty and require extensive manual programming.

Probabilistic Decision Models

Bayesian inference and Markov decision processes (MDPs) introduce probability into AI decision-making, allowing agents to assess risks, predict future states, and choose optimal actions.

Reinforcement Learning and Policy Optimization

Reinforcement learning (RL) enables agents to learn optimal decision policies through reward-driven exploration. Algorithms such as Deep Q-Networks (DQN) and Proximal Policy Optimization (PPO) allow AI to adapt in complex, dynamic environments.

Modern AI agents use a combination of these methods, allowing for situational awareness, adaptive planning, and continuous learning.

AI-Powered Robotics and Automation

The fusion of cognitive architectures with robotics and automation has transformed industries ranging from manufacturing to healthcare.

AI in Industrial Automation

Autonomous robots, powered by reinforcement learning and computer vision, are redefining production lines. Companies such as Tesla and Amazon employ robotic systems capable of real-time decision-making, quality control, and logistics optimization.

- Example: Boston Dynamics' Robotics
  Boston Dynamics' robots, such as Atlas and Spot, integrate deep learning, motion planning, and real-time perception to execute complex tasks, from parkour to hazardous site inspections.

AI in Autonomous Vehicles

Self-driving technology leverages AI cognition for environmental perception, real-time decision-making, and motion control. Companies such as Waymo and Tesla use sensor fusion and reinforcement learning to create AI agents capable of navigating unpredictable road conditions.

- Decision-Making Challenge: Autonomous vehicles must balance safety, efficiency, and ethical considerations when making split-second decisions in traffic.

AI in Healthcare Robotics

AI-driven robotic systems assist in surgery, rehabilitation, and diagnostics. Da Vinci Surgical System employs robotic precision and AI-assisted decision-making to enhance surgical outcomes. AI-powered prosthetics and exoskeletons enable adaptive movement based on neural signals.

The Future of AI Cognitive Agents

The evolution of AI cognition is accelerating toward greater autonomy, adaptability, and human-like reasoning. Key research areas include:

- Neurosymbolic AI: Enhancing interpretability while maintaining deep learning efficiency.
- Meta-Learning: AI that learns how to learn, reducing dependency on vast training datasets.
- General AI: Moving beyond task-specific models to develop universal intelligence.

AI agents that think and act are revolutionizing industries through advanced cognitive architectures, perception models, and decision-making frameworks. By integrating symbolic reasoning, neural computation, and reinforcement learning, these systems are bridging the gap between automation and true artificial cognition.

As AI continues to evolve, its ability to reason, adapt, and operate autonomously will shape the future of robotics, healthcare, transportation, and beyond. Understanding these cognitive architectures is essential for developing AI agents that are not only intelligent but also trustworthy, ethical, and capable of working alongside humans in the real world.

CHAPTER 11
Multi-Agent Systems & Swarm Intelligence

In the natural world, individual organisms often exhibit simple behaviors, yet collectively, they achieve remarkable feats. Schools of fish synchronize their movements to evade predators, flocks of birds navigate vast distances in perfect formation, and colonies of ants construct complex networks without centralized control. This phenomenon, known as swarm intelligence, has inspired a fundamental shift in artificial intelligence. Instead of a single AI agent making decisions in isolation, researchers have developed multi-agent systems (MAS) where numerous autonomous entities collaborate, compete, and adapt to solve complex problems.

Swarm intelligence and distributed AI networks have redefined fields as diverse as robotics, finance, cybersecurity, and urban planning. These systems enable decentralized decision-making, emergent intelligence, and large-scale coordination, outperforming traditional centralized models in efficiency, adaptability, and resilience. This chapter explores the core principles of multi-agent AI, the mechanics of swarm intelligence, and their transformative real-world applications, particularly in self-driving cars and smart city infrastructure.

Defining Multi-Agent Systems

A multi-agent system consists of multiple autonomous AI entities that interact in a shared environment. These agents may cooperate to achieve common goals, compete for limited resources, or operate independently with minimal communication. The defining characteristics of MAS include:

- **Autonomy**: Each agent can make independent decisions based on local data.
- **Distributed Control**: No single agent governs the system. Decisions emerge from collective interactions.
- **Communication & Adaptation**: Agents exchange information, adjust behaviors, and optimize strategies dynamically.
- **Emergent Intelligence**: The system as a whole exhibits problem-solving ability beyond the sum of individual agents.

Types of Multi-Agent Interactions

Multi-agent systems can be categorized based on their interaction dynamics:

1. Cooperative Multi-Agent Systems

In cooperative MAS, agents share a common objective and coordinate actions to achieve a unified goal. Applications include:

- **Robotic Swarms**: Teams of autonomous robots collaborating in search-and-rescue operations.
- **Healthcare AI Assistants**: AI-driven systems that jointly analyze medical data to improve diagnostics and treatment planning.

2. Competitive Multi-Agent Systems

Competitive MAS involve agents with conflicting interests, often modeled through game theory. Examples include:

- **Algorithmic Trading**: AI agents competing in high-frequency financial markets to maximize returns.
- **Cybersecurity Defense**: Adversarial AI agents detecting and countering cyber threats.

3. Hybrid Multi-Agent Systems

In hybrid MAS, agents alternate between cooperation and competition based on situational demands. A prime example is autonomous traffic systems, where vehicles coordinate to prevent congestion but also compete for optimal routes.

Architectures of Multi-Agent Systems

MAS can be structured in several ways, each with unique advantages:

1. Centralized vs. Decentralized MAS

- **Centralized MAS**: A single control unit dictates the behavior of all agents. While efficient in predictable environments, it is vulnerable to failure if the central unit is compromised.

- **Decentralized MAS**: Each agent operates independently, ensuring robustness and scalability. This model is favored in swarm robotics and distributed computing.

2. Homogeneous vs. Heterogeneous MAS

- **Homogeneous MAS**: All agents share identical capabilities and objectives, as seen in robotic swarm formations.

- **Heterogeneous MAS**: Agents have distinct roles and expertise, such as mixed AI teams in disaster response.

3. Reactive vs. Deliberative MAS

- **Reactive MAS**: Agents respond instantly to environmental stimuli, useful in high-speed decision-making scenarios like autonomous drones.
- **Deliberative MAS**: Agents engage in reasoning and planning, applied in strategic AI simulations and negotiation systems.

Fundamental Principles of Swarm Intelligence

Swarm intelligence describes a form of collective problem-solving that emerges from simple interactions among decentralized agents. Inspired by biological systems, swarm AI exhibits:

- **Self-Organization**: Agents dynamically arrange themselves without external intervention.
- **Local Decision-Making**: Each agent relies on local information rather than global knowledge.
- **Adaptive Learning**: The system continuously refines strategies based on environmental feedback.

Swarm Intelligence Algorithms

Several algorithms emulate natural swarm behavior to enhance AI decision-making:

1. Ant Colony Optimization (ACO)

Inspired by how ants find the shortest path to food, ACO is used in:

- **Network Routing**: Optimizing internet traffic flow.
- **Logistics & Supply Chains**: Enhancing warehouse management and delivery schedules.

2. Particle Swarm Optimization (PSO)

Modeled after the social behavior of birds, PSO optimizes complex functions by iteratively improving candidate solutions. Applications include:

- **Medical Imaging**: Enhancing pattern recognition in diagnostic scans.
- **Financial Forecasting**: Refining predictive models for stock market analysis.

3. Boid Flocking Model

Simulating bird flocks, the boid model is instrumental in:

- **Autonomous Drones**: Coordinating aerial navigation in search-and-rescue missions.
- **Crowd Simulation**: Enhancing pedestrian flow modeling in urban planning.

Self-Driving Cars as Multi-Agent Systems

Autonomous vehicles function as intelligent agents navigating complex, dynamic environments. Their decision-making involves:

- **Perception**: Sensors process real-time data from cameras, LiDAR, and radar.
- **Prediction**: AI forecasts traffic movements and pedestrian behavior.
- **Coordination**: Vehicles communicate with each other to optimize traffic flow.

Swarm Intelligence in Smart Cities

By integrating AI with urban infrastructure, smart cities leverage swarm intelligence to:

- **Optimize Traffic Management**: AI-controlled traffic lights adjust dynamically to minimize congestion.
- **Enhance Public Safety**: Surveillance AI detects anomalies and coordinates emergency response.
- **Improve Energy Efficiency**: Smart grids distribute electricity based on real-time demand.

The Future of Multi-Agent AI in Urban Development

Emerging innovations will refine MAS applications in smart cities, including:

- **Decentralized AI Governance**: Distributed decision-making frameworks to prevent bottlenecks.

- **Blockchain for Secure AI Transactions**: Ensuring data integrity in multi-agent collaborations.

- **Edge Computing for Real-Time Adaptation**: Reducing latency in autonomous AI operations.

The Dawn of Collective Intelligence

Multi-agent AI and swarm intelligence are redefining how machines perceive, interact, and collaborate. From autonomous vehicles navigating urban landscapes to robotic swarms revolutionizing industries, these technologies herald a new era of distributed intelligence. As research advances, AI systems will continue to evolve, blending self-learning capabilities with emergent behavior. The ultimate goal is not merely to build smarter machines but to cultivate AI ecosystems that rival the adaptability, resilience, and efficiency of nature itself.

In the age of AI-driven societies, intelligence will no longer be confined to individual machines. It will be an intricate, evolving network—an interconnected web of autonomous agents thinking, acting, and thriving together.

CHAPTER 12
AI Agents in the Real World

The integration of artificial intelligence into healthcare represents one of the most profound shifts in modern medicine. AI-driven diagnostic systems, drug discovery models, and personalized treatment plans are not mere theoretical constructs but active forces revolutionizing patient care. The evolution of AI in healthcare traces its roots back to early expert systems such as MYCIN, which utilized rule-based logic for bacterial infection diagnosis. However, with the rise of deep learning, contemporary AI models have surpassed human-level performance in specific medical tasks, offering unprecedented accuracy and efficiency.

One of the most striking examples is the application of convolutional neural networks (CNNs) in medical imaging. Studies published in *Nature Medicine* and *The Lancet* confirm that AI models can diagnose diseases such as diabetic retinopathy, melanoma, and lung cancer with accuracy matching or exceeding that of trained radiologists. Google Health's AI-driven mammography screening model, for instance, demonstrated a reduction in false negatives by 9.4 percent and false positives by 5.7 percent compared to human radiologists.

Beyond diagnostics, AI plays a critical role in drug discovery. Traditional pharmaceutical research is both time-intensive and cost-prohibitive, often requiring over a decade and billions of dollars to develop a single drug. AI-driven platforms such as DeepMind's AlphaFold have revolutionized protein folding predictions, accelerating drug design at an unprecedented scale. AI-powered generative models like Insilico Medicine's *Chemistry42* can generate novel molecular structures optimized for specific biological targets, significantly reducing research timelines.

Personalized medicine represents the next frontier, where AI tailors treatments based on an individual's genetic, environmental, and lifestyle factors. AI agents analyze genomic data to predict disease susceptibility and optimize drug prescriptions, minimizing adverse reactions. IBM Watson, despite its commercial setbacks, demonstrated AI's potential to assist oncologists by cross-referencing thousands of medical studies in seconds to recommend optimal cancer treatments.

While AI's contributions to healthcare are revolutionary, ethical considerations remain paramount. Issues such as algorithmic bias, data privacy, and the interpretability of black-box models necessitate rigorous oversight to ensure AI-driven healthcare remains equitable and transparent.

AI in Finance: Algorithmic Trading and Risk Management

The financial sector has long been a proving ground for AI's capabilities. Algorithmic trading, credit risk assessment, fraud detection, and portfolio optimization have all been transformed by intelligent agents. Unlike human traders, AI-powered systems process vast amounts of market data, identify hidden patterns, and execute trades in milliseconds.

High-frequency trading (HFT) firms such as Citadel Securities and Renaissance Technologies rely on AI-driven algorithms that leverage reinforcement learning and deep neural networks to predict market fluctuations with unparalleled precision. These models analyze vast datasets encompassing historical prices, news sentiment, and even satellite imagery of store parking lots to infer economic activity.

Beyond trading, AI significantly enhances risk management. Banks and hedge funds employ AI models to assess credit risk by analyzing unconventional data sources, such as social media behavior and transaction history. Neural networks outperform traditional credit-scoring models by identifying nuanced correlations that human analysts might overlook.

JPMorgan's AI-powered *LOXM* system, for instance, optimizes trade execution strategies by continuously learning from past market conditions.

Fraud detection is another domain where AI has proven indispensable. Machine learning models trained on millions of financial transactions identify anomalies indicative of fraud with remarkable accuracy. Mastercard's Decision Intelligence platform, for example, detects fraudulent transactions in real-time, significantly reducing financial losses.

Despite AI's advancements in finance, its deployment is not without risk. Algorithmic trading can exacerbate market volatility, as seen in the 2010 Flash Crash, where automated trading systems triggered a rapid market collapse. Ensuring transparency and regulatory compliance remains a critical challenge in AI-driven finance.

AI in Cybersecurity: Threat Detection and Prevention

The cybersecurity landscape has evolved into a digital battlefield where AI functions as both a defensive shield and an offensive weapon. Traditional rule-based security systems struggle to keep pace with the rapidly evolving tactics of cybercriminals, necessitating AI-driven approaches.

Machine learning models now power threat detection systems capable of identifying malware, phishing attempts, and advanced persistent threats (APTs) before they execute. AI-driven anomaly detection identifies deviations from normal network behavior, enabling real-time threat mitigation. Darktrace's *Enterprise Immune System*, inspired by biological immune responses, autonomously detects and neutralizes cyber threats by continuously adapting to new attack vectors.

Deep learning models enhance AI's ability to detect sophisticated cyber threats. Generative adversarial networks (GANs) simulate cyberattacks, allowing AI-driven security platforms to train against ever-evolving threats. Google's Chronicle, an AI-powered cybersecurity platform, processes petabytes of security telemetry data to uncover hidden attack patterns.

However, the dual-use nature of AI poses significant risks. Adversarial AI, where attackers manipulate machine learning models to evade detection, presents an ongoing challenge. Deepfake technology, capable of generating hyper-realistic audio and video for social engineering attacks, exemplifies AI's potential for cybercrime.

To combat these threats, AI-driven security frameworks must incorporate explainability and adversarial robustness.

Organizations must balance AI automation with human oversight to ensure ethical cybersecurity practices.

AI's Role in Predictive Policing

The application of AI in law enforcement, particularly predictive policing, has sparked significant debate. Predictive policing systems analyze historical crime data to forecast where crimes are likely to occur and, in some cases, identify individuals at higher risk of committing offenses. While proponents argue that AI can enhance public safety, critics warn of algorithmic bias and ethical dilemmas.

One of the most widely studied predictive policing systems is PredPol, which uses machine learning to predict crime hotspots based on historical incident reports. The system has been implemented in multiple U.S. cities, claiming to optimize law enforcement resource allocation. However, studies have revealed that predictive models trained on biased historical data often reinforce systemic disparities, disproportionately targeting minority communities.

Facial recognition AI, another controversial law enforcement tool, has been deployed by agencies worldwide to identify suspects in real-time. China's extensive surveillance network employs AI-powered facial recognition to monitor public spaces, raising concerns about privacy violations and mass surveillance.

Despite its flaws, AI has also been used to exonerate the wrongfully convicted. Projects such as the Innocence Project leverage machine learning to analyze forensic evidence, leading to overturned convictions in cases of wrongful imprisonment.

The future of AI in law enforcement depends on the establishment of ethical guidelines, transparency, and oversight mechanisms. Without proper safeguards, predictive policing risks becoming a tool for perpetuating injustice rather than preventing crime.

Conclusion

AI agents are no longer confined to research laboratories and theoretical discussions. They are actively shaping industries, revolutionizing medicine, finance, cybersecurity, and law enforcement. The depth and breadth of AI's impact demand continuous evaluation, ensuring that its deployment aligns with ethical principles, regulatory standards, and societal well-being.

As AI continues to evolve, the central question remains: how can humanity harness its full potential while mitigating its inherent risks? The answer lies in responsible AI development, interdisciplinary collaboration, and a commitment to balancing innovation with accountability.

CHAPTER 13
Deploying AI Agents in Production

The development of artificial intelligence agents has reached an inflection point where theoretical advancements must transition into scalable, production-ready systems. While AI research has yielded groundbreaking models in natural language processing, computer vision, and decision-making, the challenge lies in deploying these agents into real-world environments with high reliability, adaptability, and efficiency.

Enterprise applications demand robust architectures capable of handling vast datasets, dynamic user interactions, and mission-critical decision-making processes. This chapter explores the key considerations for deploying AI agents at scale, leveraging cloud platforms, and implementing continuous performance monitoring. It provides a structured framework for organizations to transition from experimental AI models to fully operational systems that drive measurable business value.

Scaling AI for Enterprise Applications

1. Architectural Considerations for Scalable AI

Successful AI deployment requires more than a well-trained model. It demands a resilient architecture that ensures computational efficiency, fault tolerance, and scalability. Organizations must consider the following architectural principles when integrating AI agents into production environments:

- **Microservices Architecture**: AI models should be modular, allowing for independent scaling of different components. For example, a recommendation system might consist of separate services for data preprocessing, model inference, and real-time decision-making.

- **Containerization and Orchestration**: Docker and Kubernetes enable AI models to be deployed consistently across diverse environments while providing automated scaling and load balancing.

- **Latency Optimization**: In applications such as fraud detection and autonomous systems, inference speed is critical. Optimizations using techniques like quantization, pruning, and model distillation can reduce computational overhead.

- **Fault Tolerance and Redundancy**: High-availability AI systems must have built-in redundancies, allowing for seamless failover mechanisms in case of hardware or software failures.

2. Data Pipeline Engineering

AI agents thrive on high-quality, continuously updated data streams. The deployment of AI systems requires well-structured data pipelines capable of handling:

- **Real-Time Data Processing**: AI applications in finance and cybersecurity require immediate insights. Technologies such as Apache Kafka and Apache Flink enable streaming data ingestion.

- **Batch Processing for Model Training**: Enterprise AI relies on batch-processing frameworks like Apache Spark to train models on historical datasets while optimizing computational efficiency.

- **Data Versioning and Governance**: Tools like DVC (Data Version Control) and MLflow track dataset changes, ensuring reproducibility and regulatory compliance.

3. Model Serving and API Deployment

Once trained, AI models must be accessible to enterprise applications through standardized interfaces. Model deployment strategies include:

- **RESTful and gRPC APIs**: AI models can be exposed as services through API frameworks like FastAPI and TensorFlow Serving, enabling seamless integration with existing enterprise applications.

- **Edge AI Deployment**: For applications requiring on-device inference, such as autonomous drones and IoT devices, frameworks like TensorFlow Lite and NVIDIA Jetson enable efficient edge computing.

- **Hybrid Cloud Deployment**: Organizations often adopt a hybrid approach, combining on-premise infrastructure with cloud-based AI services to balance data security and computational scalability.

Cloud Deployment: AWS, Google Cloud, and Azure AI

Cloud platforms provide enterprises with the infrastructure, scalability, and security needed to deploy AI agents at scale. Each major cloud provider offers specialized AI services, including managed model deployment, automated monitoring, and seamless integration with enterprise workflows.

1. Amazon Web Services (AWS) for AI Deployment

AWS offers a robust AI ecosystem, making it a preferred choice for large-scale AI deployments. Key services include:

- **Amazon SageMaker**: Provides an end-to-end solution for training, tuning, and deploying AI models with built-in auto-scaling and monitoring.

- **AWS Lambda for AI Inference**: Enables serverless execution of AI models, reducing infrastructure management overhead.

- **Amazon Comprehend and Recognition**: Pre-trained AI models for NLP and computer vision tasks allow businesses to leverage AI without extensive model training.

2. Google Cloud AI & TensorFlow Extended (TFX)

Google Cloud is renowned for its deep learning capabilities, offering AI services optimized for large-scale deployments:

- **Vertex AI**: An enterprise-grade AI development and deployment platform that simplifies model training and serving.

- **TensorFlow Extended (TFX)**: A comprehensive framework for managing ML pipelines, ensuring reproducibility, and integrating with Kubernetes.

- **AutoML and TPUs**: Google Cloud AutoML enables non-experts to train custom models, while Tensor Processing Units (TPUs) accelerate AI workloads beyond traditional GPUs.

3. Microsoft Azure AI and ML Services

Azure provides enterprise-ready AI solutions with seamless integration into Microsoft's ecosystem:

- **Azure Machine Learning (Azure ML)**: A unified platform for model training, deployment, and monitoring, supporting both code-first and low-code AI development.

- **Azure Cognitive Services**: A suite of pre-trained AI models for speech recognition, sentiment analysis, and anomaly detection.

- **Azure Synapse Analytics**: Enables enterprises to integrate AI models with data warehouses for predictive analytics at scale.

How to Monitor and Maintain AI Agent Performance

1. Continuous Model Evaluation and Drift Detection

AI models degrade over time due to changing data distributions, requiring continuous monitoring to maintain accuracy and reliability. Best practices include:

- **Concept Drift Detection**: Techniques such as statistical hypothesis testing and adaptive learning models help detect shifts in input data distribution.

- **Real-Time Model Auditing**: Logging AI predictions and monitoring discrepancies between expected and actual outcomes ensures ongoing performance validation.

- **A/B Testing for AI Models**: Deploying multiple AI models in parallel allows organizations to compare performance before making full-scale changes.

2. Explainability and Interpretability in AI Agents

As AI agents take on increasingly complex decision-making roles, organizations must prioritize interpretability to ensure transparency and regulatory compliance:

- **SHAP (Shapley Additive explanations)**: Provides insight into how AI models generate predictions by assigning feature importance scores.

- **LIME (Local Interpretable Model-Agnostic Explanations)**: Generates human-readable explanations for individual AI model decisions.

- **Counterfactual Explanations**: Helps users understand how slight input modifications would alter AI-generated predictions.

3. Security and Ethical Considerations in AI Deployment

Deployed AI agents must be secured against adversarial attacks and biased decision-making. Organizations should implement:

- **Adversarial Defense Mechanisms**: Techniques such as adversarial training and defensive distillation help protect AI models from malicious input manipulations.

- **Bias Mitigation Strategies**: Fairness-aware model training techniques, such as reweighting and adversarial debiasing, ensure equitable AI decision-making.

- **Compliance with AI Regulations**: AI deployment must adhere to global regulatory frameworks such as GDPR, CCPA, and ISO/IEC 42001 AI governance standards.

The Future of AI Deployment in Enterprise Systems

Deploying AI agents in production is no longer an experimental endeavor but a strategic imperative for organizations seeking competitive advantage. As AI adoption accelerates, enterprises must invest in scalable architectures, cloud-based AI ecosystems, and continuous performance monitoring to ensure long-term success.

Future AI deployment trends will likely include fully autonomous AI agents capable of self-optimization, federated learning architectures for privacy-preserving model training, and neuromorphic computing paradigms that mimic human cognitive processes. Organizations that master AI deployment today will define the technological landscape of tomorrow.

This chapter has provided a comprehensive roadmap for transitioning AI agents from research prototypes to enterprise-grade production systems. By leveraging best practices in AI architecture, cloud deployment, and performance monitoring, organizations can unlock the full potential of AI-driven transformation.

CHAPTER 14
The Ethics of AI and Bias Mitigation

Artificial intelligence is reshaping every facet of human existence, from decision-making in healthcare and finance to surveillance and autonomous weapons systems. As AI systems gain increasing autonomy, they inherit not only the computational efficiency of their architectures but also the biases, ethical dilemmas, and moral failures of the data and algorithms that power them.

AI bias is no longer a theoretical concern confined to research papers and philosophical debates. It manifests in real-world consequences, such as discriminatory hiring algorithms, racially biased facial recognition, and AI-driven credit assessments that systematically disadvantage certain demographics. If left unchecked, AI bias could reinforce systemic inequalities, erode public trust, and undermine the very institutions it aims to enhance.

This chapter explores the dangers of AI bias, the ethical and legal frameworks governing AI, and the strategies required to build transparent, fair, and accountable AI systems.

The Dangers of AI Bias and How to Prevent It

1. Understanding AI Bias: Origins and Manifestations

Bias in artificial intelligence arises from multiple sources, including biased training data, flawed model design, and misaligned objectives. It can manifest in different ways, such as:

- **Historical Bias**: When AI models learn from past data reflecting social inequalities, they perpetuate those disparities. For example, an AI recruitment system trained on historical hiring patterns may favor male candidates over equally qualified female applicants.

- **Algorithmic Bias**: When certain subgroups are systematically disadvantaged due to the mathematical properties of an AI model. A well-known case involved facial recognition algorithms that misclassified darker-skinned individuals at a much higher rate than lighter-skinned individuals.

- **Sample Bias**: When training datasets fail to represent diverse populations, leading to inaccurate predictions for underrepresented groups. Medical AI systems trained primarily on data from European populations have been found to perform poorly on African and Asian patients.

- **Labeling Bias**: When human-annotated training data introduces subjective or prejudiced categorizations, leading to skewed AI outputs. Sentiment analysis models, for example, have been shown to label African American Vernacular English (AAVE) as more negative than standard American English.

2. Case Studies: When AI Bias Had Real-World Consequences

- **COMPAS and Criminal Justice Bias**
  The COMPAS (Correctional Offender Management Profiling for Alternative Sanctions) algorithm, used in the United States to assess criminal recidivism risk, was found to falsely label Black defendants as high risk at twice the rate of white defendants. This resulted in longer sentences and harsher bail conditions, exacerbating racial disparities in the criminal justice system.

- **Amazon's Biased Hiring Algorithm**
  Amazon developed an AI-powered hiring tool to streamline recruitment. However, the system was found to systematically downgrade applications containing the word "women's" (such as

"women's chess club") due to historical hiring data favoring male candidates. Amazon ultimately scrapped the project.

- **Healthcare AI Discrimination** A widely used healthcare algorithm was found to allocate less medical care to Black patients compared to equally sick white patients because it relied on historical healthcare spending as a proxy for medical need. Since Black patients had historically lower healthcare expenditures due to systemic inequalities, the AI mistakenly inferred that they required less care.

3. Strategies to Prevent AI Bias

To mitigate bias and build fair AI systems, organizations must adopt a multi-faceted approach:

- **Bias Audits and Fairness Testing** Implementing fairness metrics such as disparate impact analysis, equalized odds, and demographic parity ensures AI models do not disproportionately disadvantage specific groups.
- **Diverse and Representative Training Data** Ensuring that datasets include a balanced representation of gender, race, and socioeconomic

groups reduces the risk of biased predictions. Techniques such as data augmentation and synthetic data generation can be used to balance datasets.

- **Algorithmic Transparency and Explainability**
  Black-box AI systems must be replaced with interpretable models that allow stakeholders to understand how decisions are made. Tools such as SHAP (Shapley Additive explanations) and LIME (Local Interpretable Model-Agnostic Explanations) provide insights into model behavior.

- **Human-In-the-Loop   Systems**
  AI systems should incorporate human oversight in high-stakes decision-making to prevent automated biases from leading to harmful outcomes. In medical diagnostics, for example, AI recommendations should be reviewed by human experts before final decisions are made.

- **Regulatory Compliance and Ethical AI Governance**
  Organizations must align their AI practices with ethical AI principles, ensuring compliance with global regulations. AI ethics boards and external audits can help enforce these standards.

AI and the Law: Understanding Regulations and Compliance

As AI technology advances, governments worldwide are enacting legal frameworks to regulate its use. Ethical AI development is no longer optional—it is a legal obligation.

1. Global AI Regulations and Their Implications

- **European Union's AI Act**

  The EU's Artificial Intelligence Act categorizes AI systems into four risk levels: unacceptable, high-risk, limited-risk, and minimal-risk. High-risk AI systems, such as biometric identification and credit scoring models, must adhere to strict transparency and accountability standards.

- **United States AI Policies**

  While the U.S. lacks a unified AI regulation, agencies such as the Federal Trade Commission (FTC) and the Equal Employment Opportunity Commission (EEOC) are increasingly scrutinizing AI-driven discrimination and unfair business practices.

- **China's AI Governance Model**

  China has implemented regulations requiring AI companies to align their models with socialist values and national security interests. Algorithmic recommendations and deepfake technology are strictly monitored.

- **GDPR and AI Compliance**

  The General Data Protection Regulation (GDPR) mandates that AI systems provide explainability, fairness, and the right to contest automated decisions. Organizations using AI for consumer-related applications must ensure transparency and user control over data.

2. Legal Challenges and Ethical Dilemmas

- **AI Liability and Accountability**

  If an AI-driven medical system makes a misdiagnosis leading to patient harm, who is responsible? Current legal frameworks struggle to assign liability in AI-driven errors.

- **Bias and Discrimination Lawsuits**

  Companies deploying biased AI models have faced legal challenges, as seen in the case of facial recognition companies sued for racial profiling and data privacy violations.

- **AI in Warfare and Autonomous Weapons**

  The use of AI-driven autonomous weapons

raises ethical concerns regarding human oversight and decision-making in life-or-death situations. The United Nations has called for an international ban on lethal autonomous weapons systems.

How to Build Ethical AI Systems

1. Implementing Ethical AI Design Principles

Building ethical AI systems requires integrating ethical considerations at every stage of development. Organizations should adopt the following principles:

- **Fairness and Non-Discrimination**: AI must be designed to ensure equal treatment across demographic groups.
- **Transparency and Explainability**: AI decision-making processes must be interpretable by users and stakeholders.
- **Privacy and Data Protection**: AI systems must safeguard personal data, adhering to data minimization and encryption standards.
- **Human-Centric AI**: AI should augment human decision-making rather than replace critical human oversight.

2. Developing a Standardized Ethical AI Framework

A structured ethical AI framework should include:

- **Bias Mitigation Protocols**: Regular audits and fairness assessments before model deployment.
- **Ethical AI Certification**: Independent verification ensuring AI models comply with ethical and legal standards.
- **Continuous Ethical Training for AI Practitioners**: Educating AI developers on the societal impact of biased models.

The Future of Ethical AI

The ethical challenges of AI are not merely technical—they are societal, legal, and philosophical. As AI systems become more powerful, their impact on human lives intensifies. Organizations must take a proactive approach in ensuring fairness, accountability, and transparency in AI deployment.

By implementing robust bias mitigation strategies, complying with evolving legal frameworks, and embedding ethics into AI design, we can build a future where AI serves humanity rather than exacerbates its divisions. Ethical AI is not just an aspiration—it is an imperative.

CHAPTER 15
The Future of AI Agent Development

For decades, artificial intelligence has evolved within the constraints of specialized problem-solving, excelling at narrow tasks yet remaining fundamentally limited in adaptability. This paradigm, often referred to as narrow AI (ANI—Artificial Narrow Intelligence), has shaped industries, redefined automation, and propelled computational efficiency to unprecedented heights. However, the next frontier lies in the pursuit of Artificial General Intelligence (AGI)—a system capable of understanding, reasoning, and adapting across diverse domains with human-like cognitive flexibility.

AGI represents not merely an incremental improvement but a radical shift in computational intelligence. Unlike its narrow counterpart, AGI aspires to integrate abstract reasoning, self-improvement, and cross-domain learning. It has the potential to revolutionize scientific discovery, economic systems, and even our philosophical understanding of consciousness and intelligence.

This chapter delves into the computational foundations, emergent challenges, and ethical implications of AGI. It examines the interdisciplinary insights from neuroscience, cognitive psychology, and computational modeling that inform AGI development. It also explores the role of multiagent collaboration, hierarchical learning architectures, and self-improving reinforcement models in the evolution toward true artificial general intelligence.

The Foundations of AGI

The quest for AGI requires a synthesis of multiple computational paradigms. While deep learning and neural networks have dominated recent advancements, achieving general intelligence demands a more comprehensive approach, integrating the following frameworks:

1. Symbolic AI vs. Subsymbolic AI

AGI necessitates a reconciliation between symbolic reasoning (explicit rule-based logic) and subsymbolic approaches (pattern recognition through neural networks). Symbolic AI, rooted in the early works of John McCarthy and Marvin Minsky, provides structured reasoning and knowledge representation, while subsymbolic AI, championed by Geoffrey Hinton and Yann LeCun, enables fluid pattern recognition and learning. Modern AGI research explores hybrid models that integrate both, such as neuro-symbolic AI, which combines symbolic logic with deep learning architectures.

2. Centralized vs. Distributed Intelligence

Traditional AI models rely on centralized architectures, where learning occurs within a singular system. However, AGI may require distributed intelligence, leveraging multi-agent systems that collaborate, communicate, and collectively refine knowledge. Distributed cognition, inspired by biological swarms and human collective intelligence, enhances adaptability and problem-solving efficiency.

3. Self-Supervised Learning and Emergent Intelligence

Self-supervised learning represents a crucial step toward AGI, allowing models to infer patterns from raw data without labeled supervision. This approach, explored in models such as DeepMind's AlphaZero and OpenAI's GPT series, enhances an AI system's ability to generalize knowledge across tasks. Emergent intelligence—where sophisticated behaviors arise from simple rules—has been observed in reinforcement learning agents, demonstrating AGI's potential to evolve beyond programmed constraints.

4. Recursive Self-Improvement and Meta-Learning

One of the defining characteristics of AGI will be its capacity for recursive self-improvement—modifying its own algorithms to enhance efficiency, decision-making, and reasoning. Meta-learning, or "learning to learn," accelerates this process by enabling AI systems to dynamically adapt to novel challenges with minimal data input.

AGI: Breakthroughs and Challenges

1. Neuroscientific Insights into General Intelligence

Neuroscientists have long studied the cognitive mechanisms underlying human intelligence. Theories such as the Global Workspace Theory (GWT) by Bernard Baars suggest that consciousness arises from a distributed cognitive framework, where multiple specialized modules integrate information. AGI research increasingly draws upon such insights to develop architectures that mirror human cognition, integrating memory, attention, and abstraction.

2. Embodied AI and Sensorimotor Learning

A purely digital AGI may struggle with real-world adaptability. Embodied AI—robots or virtual agents that interact physically with their environment—enhances learning through sensory experiences, akin to human cognition. Sensorimotor learning, exemplified in humanoid robots such as Boston Dynamics' Atlas, allows AI to develop spatial reasoning, dexterity, and real-time decision-making.

3. The Alignment Problem and Ethical Constraints

Ensuring AGI aligns with human values is one of the most critical challenges in AI safety research. The alignment problem, highlighted by AI theorists such as Stuart Russell and Nick Bostrom, questions whether an advanced AI will act in accordance with human intent. Strategies such as inverse reinforcement learning (IRL) and constitutional AI aim to encode ethical considerations into AGI models.

4. Computational and Hardware Limitations

Despite algorithmic advancements, AGI development is constrained by computational resources. Quantum computing offers a potential breakthrough, with its ability to process vast probabilistic calculations in parallel. Neuromorphic computing, which emulates brain-like neural architectures, presents another promising avenue for AGI scalability.

AI and Human Collaboration

While AGI is often portrayed as a competitor to human intelligence, its true potential lies in collaboration. AI-augmented cognition—where AI enhances human problem-solving, creativity, and decision-making—presents a vision of mutual advancement rather than displacement. The following domains illustrate AI-human synergy:

1. Scientific Discovery and Innovation

AI-driven scientific discovery accelerates research in medicine, materials science, and theoretical physics. DeepMind's AlphaFold has already revolutionized protein folding predictions, showcasing AI's role in biological breakthroughs. AGI could further assist in unifying physics theories or developing novel materials with properties beyond human intuition.

2. Personalized AI Companions and Assistants

Future AGI-powered assistants will transcend current chatbot capabilities, offering real-time emotional intelligence, context-aware decision support, and personalized coaching. These systems will integrate cognitive psychology principles, enhancing user productivity, learning, and well-being.

3. AI in Governance and Policy Decision-Making

Governments and policymakers could leverage AI to simulate economic models, predict crises, and optimize resource distribution. However, transparency and accountability will be crucial to prevent algorithmic biases and ethical dilemmas in decision-making processes.

How to Stay Ahead in AI Development

Given the rapid advancements in AI, continuous learning and adaptation are essential for researchers, engineers, and entrepreneurs. The following strategies will ensure relevance in the evolving AI landscape:

1. Mastering AI Fundamentals and Emerging Paradigms

A deep understanding of machine learning, reinforcement learning, and neural networks remains foundational. Exploring cutting-edge research, including transformer architectures and self-supervised learning models, will provide a competitive edge.

2. Hands-On Implementation and Experimentation

Engaging in practical AI development—experimenting with open-source frameworks such as TensorFlow, PyTorch, and JAX—enhances theoretical knowledge. Participating in AI competitions and contributing to research papers strengthens expertise.

3. Interdisciplinary Learning and Ethical AI Development

The future of AI will be shaped by interdisciplinary collaboration. Understanding cognitive science, neuroscience, and philosophy will inform more holistic AGI architectures. Additionally, staying informed on AI ethics, regulatory frameworks, and responsible AI design is critical.

4. Building and Contributing to Open AI Communities

Engagement with open-source AI communities, such as Hugging Face and OpenAI forums, fosters knowledge exchange and collaborative innovation. Contributing to AI safety initiatives and fairness frameworks ensures AI development aligns with ethical considerations.

A Future Defined by Intelligence

The trajectory of AI development points toward a future where intelligence—both artificial and human—converges in unprecedented ways. The realization of AGI will redefine industries, transform economies, and challenge the very nature of human cognition. However, the true measure of success will not merely be in creating superintelligent machines but in ensuring these systems serve humanity's highest aspirations.

Understanding AGI requires not just technical expertise but also a philosophical re-examination of intelligence itself. As we stand at the threshold of this new era, the challenge before us is not merely to build AGI but to shape it in ways that enhance human potential, wisdom, and collective progress.

APPENDICES

Books

These books provide a strong theoretical foundation, practical guidance, and insights into the evolution of AI:

1. **"Artificial Intelligence: A Guide for Thinking Humans"** – Melanie Mitchell
2. **"Superintelligence: Paths, Dangers, Strategies"** – Nick Bostrom
3. **"The Book of Why: The New Science of Cause and Effect"** – Judea Pearl and Dana Mackenzie
4. **"Deep Learning"** – Ian Goodfellow, Yoshua Bengio, and Aaron Courville
5. **"Reinforcement Learning: An Introduction"** – Richard S. Sutton and Andrew G. Barto
6. **"Life 3.0: Being Human in the Age of Artificial Intelligence"** – Max Tegmark
7. **"Grokking Deep Learning"** – Andrew W. Trask
8. **"The Master Algorithm: How the Quest for the Ultimate Learning Machine Will Remake Our World"** – Pedro Domingos

9. **"Neural Networks and Deep Learning"** – Michael Nielsen

10. **"Artificial Intelligence: Foundations of Computational Agents"** – David Poole and Alan Mackworth

Courses

These courses cover everything from foundational AI principles to cutting-edge deep learning techniques:

1. **CS50's Introduction to Artificial Intelligence with Python** – Harvard (edX)

2. **Machine Learning Specialization** – Andrew Ng (Coursera, DeepLearning.AI)

3. **Deep Learning Specialization** – Andrew Ng (Coursera, DeepLearning.AI)

4. **Fast.ai's Practical Deep Learning for Coders** – Jeremy Howard (Fast.ai)

5. **MIT's Introduction to Deep Learning (6.S191)** – MIT OpenCourseWare

6. **Reinforcement Learning Specialization** – David Silver (DeepMind, UCL)

7. **Generative Adversarial Networks (GANs) Specialization** – DeepLearning.AI (Coursera)

8. **Natural Language Processing Specialization** – DeepLearning.AI (Coursera)

9. **Advanced AI for Healthcare** – Stanford AI Lab (Stanford Online)

10. **AI Ethics and Society** – Carnegie Mellon University (Open Learning Initiative)

Research Papers and Whitepapers

These foundational and cutting-edge research papers provide essential knowledge on AI's evolution:

1. **"Computing Machinery and Intelligence"** – Alan Turing (1950)

2. **"A Logical Calculus of Ideas Immanent in Nervous Activity"** – Warren McCulloch and Walter Pitts (1943)

3. **"Perceptrons: An Introduction to Computational Geometry"** – Marvin Minsky and Seymour Papert (1969)

4. **"Learning Representations by Backpropagating Errors"** – David Rumelhart, Geoffrey Hinton, and Ronald Williams (1986)

5. **"Playing Atari with Deep Reinforcement Learning"** – DeepMind (2013)

6. **"Auto-Encoding Variational Bayes"** – Kingma and Welling (2013)

7. **"Attention Is All You Need"** – Vaswani et al. (2017)

8. **"Mastering Chess and Shogi by Self-Play with a General Reinforcement Learning Algorithm"** – DeepMind (2017)

9. **"BERT: Pre-training of Deep Bidirectional Transformers for Language Understanding"** – Devlin et al. (2018)

10. **"GPT-4 Technical Report"** – OpenAI (2023)

AI Development Roadmap – From Beginner to Expert

Beginner Level (0-6 months)

- Learn Python, NumPy, Pandas, and Matplotlib
- Understand basic machine learning concepts (supervised, unsupervised, reinforcement learning)
- Complete Andrew Ng's Machine Learning Course
- Implement basic models using Scikit-learn and TensorFlow

Intermediate Level (6-18 months)

- Deep dive into deep learning (CNNs, RNNs, Transformers)
- Work with PyTorch and TensorFlow for neural network implementation
- Study reinforcement learning and GANs
- Build real-world AI applications (image classification, sentiment analysis)

Advanced Level (18+ months)

- Explore meta-learning and self-supervised learning
- Develop multi-agent AI systems and hierarchical reinforcement learning models
- Study AI safety, interpretability, and ethics
- Contribute to AI research papers and open-source AI projects

Glossary of Key AI Terms

A

- **Adversarial Networks (GANs)** – Neural networks designed to generate realistic data through competition between a generator and a discriminator.

- **Agent-Based Models** – AI models in which multiple agents interact with their environment and each other.

B

- **Backpropagation** – A method for training neural networks by adjusting weights based on error gradients.
- **Bayesian Networks** – Probabilistic graphical models used for inference in uncertain environments.

C

- **CNN (Convolutional Neural Network)** – A deep learning model designed for image recognition.
- **Causal Inference** – A method for determining cause-effect relationships in AI.

D

- **Deep Learning** – A subset of machine learning using multi-layered neural networks.
- **Diffusion Models** – Generative models used for high-quality image and text generation.

156

R

- **Reinforcement Learning (RL)** – A learning paradigm where agents maximize cumulative rewards.

- **ResNet** – A deep learning model designed to handle very deep networks through residual learning.

ABOUT THE AUTHOR

Hi, I'm Orion Steele, an AI enthusiast, developer, and futurist with a passion for engineering intelligence. My journey into artificial intelligence began with an insatiable curiosity about how machines learn, think, and evolve. Over the years, I have dedicated myself to mastering AI agent development, exploring the frontiers of automation, deep learning, and autonomous systems.

When I am not immersed in AI research or writing, you will find me experimenting with new technologies, engaging in thought-provoking discussions about the future of AI, or mentoring others on their own paths to mastery. Through my work, I aim to bridge the gap between cutting-edge AI advancements and practical implementation, empowering others to build intelligent systems that shape the world.

This book is a culmination of my experience, insights, and lessons learned. It is designed to take you from novice to expert in AI agent development. Welcome to the journey.